A Japanese I ~~p~~ ~~~~ ~~~~
Daughter

A Japanese Diplomat's Daughter

◆

An Outsider's Childhood in the 1930s and 1940s

Ayako Tomii

iUniverse, Inc.

New York Lincoln Shanghai

A Japanese Diplomat's Daughter
An Outsider's Childhood in the 1930s and 1940s

iUniverse, Inc.

For information address:
iUniverse, Inc.
2021 Pine Lake Road, Suite 100
Lincoln, NE 68512
www.iuniverse.com

ISBN: 0-595-29800-1

Contents

JAPAN

Oranges

It was winter in Tokyo, 1934. A crate of oranges had just arrived from my father, the new consul general in San Francisco, and the fragrance filled the room. This is the earliest picture in my mind. Snuggled up to my mother, who was a great beauty by Western standards, with her large, deep-set eyes, I watched my brother make a snowman in the garden. Masa was nine and had just come back from school. We lived in a traditional Japanese house, with sliding glass doors the length of the garden, and I could see the snow falling, the trees covered with white stillness.

"Masa, come and see what your father's sent us! Surprise!" Snowflakes rushed in with the cold wind as Mama opened a glass door; she clutched the front of her purple and white kimono and shivered.

"I want to finish my snowman first!"

"*Okusama*! Madam! May we see too? We've never seen oranges." The maids, O-Natsu and Fusa, squatted in the corridor, as excited as the children.

"Since *Obotchama*, the young master, doesn't seem curious, shall we peek first?" Mama replied, sitting beside me on her cushion. O-Natsu opened the crate in a flurry of hammer and nails and scissors and rope and giggles. Fusa, quieter, sat apart from us, tidying away the mess. She had come only a week ago and was to go with Mama and me to San Francisco.

"Oh. Mmm…"

"Ah. Mmm…"

"This is eaten every day over there?"

Mama took out three oranges. "Beautiful, and from so far away. First I must offer these to our ancestors," she said, as she placed the three in front of the miniature shrine in the room. She joined her hands in prayer and bowed. "From Shu; all of you must be so proud of him; he honors the family name." Mama took out more oranges. "Two for Masa, one for you, Ayako, one for O-Natsu, one for Fusa, one for the cook, and one for me."

"Oh, thank you, *Okusama*." O-Natsu turned her orange round and round, then smelled it. She had two silver teeth in front, of which she was very proud; she was a country girl with ruddy cheeks and cheerful disposition. "It's the first

3

time I've seen an orange. Fusa, how lucky you are, going over to A-me-ri-ca with *Okusama* and *Ojohsama*, our little miss."

"Yes, you'll be able to pluck oranges every day from your window, Fusa!" Mama repeated what Papa had written her.

"I hope I won't get seasick," Fusa said, looking worried.

Sniffing my orange, I thought of Papa—tall, laughing Papa—and wondered what it would be like to see him again. Fusa was to look after me, but I liked O-Natsu better. "I wish you were coming with us instead of Fusa!"

O-Natsu giggled, her silver teeth twinkling through her fingers as she covered her mouth shyly, her cheeks flaming like apples. "Hee hee hee, you shouldn't say such things, *Ojohsama*. I'm just a country girl, but Fusa, she's educated—her father's a teacher. Fusa's the right person to go with you."

Snowflakes and a blast of cold air blew in as Masa opened the glass doors and came inside, shaking the snow off his cap, jacket, and mittens. He stood tall, with a high forehead like Papa's and deep-set eyes like Mama's. "Oh, you've already opened the box?"

"We couldn't wait to see. Here are two oranges for you—don't they smell marvelous? They're so much larger than our tangerines. I must take some to your Grandfather and Grandmother Tomii. But then," Mama smiled, "being your father, he's probably sent them a box already. I'll give some to your aunts and uncles and to Grandma Nakamura. Your father is so extravagant."

Masa fingered his oranges and looked glum. "Why can't I go to San Francisco like you and Ayako?"

The maids closed the paper doors to the corridor and vanished.

Mama sighed. "I wish you could. You came with us to Canada and spoke such good English, which you've now forgotten. But I've told you over and over again, when Japanese boys reach school age they have to remain in their country and receive a Japanese education."

"I want to be with you and Papa. It's not fair that Ayako gets to go."

"And I wish you could come, too. Ayako's only four, and besides, girls don't have to find jobs like boys do. You have lots of friends at school whom you wouldn't want to leave, and besides, you'll be living with your Grandfather and Grandmother Tomii. From next month, in fact, we'll all be moving into your grandparents' house before we leave for San Francisco."

Masa sulked. "Grandma Nakamura isn't so bad—I wouldn't mind staying with her—but Grandma Tomii's a fusspot." Also, Grandma Nakamura was a widow, and that meant there would be one less grownup to keep an eye on him.

"Your father's the eldest son, so of course you, being the son of the eldest, should stay with the Tomii grandparents and not Grandmama Nakamura. You are a Tomii and not a Nakamura."

"What's a fusspot, Mama?"

Grandfather and Grandmother Tomii

In March we moved to Yakuohji-machi in Ushigome-ku, and Fusa came with us. O-Natsu had gone back to Gifu Prefecture to prepare for her September wedding, for Mama had found a husband for O-Natsu (Jiro-san, the local bicycle shop owner's second son). Our departure had been delayed and Mama had been a dutiful daughter-in-law for three months already.

I liked the mystery of the rambling house, with its gardens. A large gravel courtyard led to the Western-style left wing, with its dignified entrance. A bamboo fence hid the garden that led to the entrance to the middle and right wings. Corridors connected the wings on the ground floor only, which meant great distances and possibilities for tag up and down the stairs. The entire house, with its many forbidden rooms, seemed made for hide-and-seek on rainy days. The left wing housed the dark parlour and library, with their stuffed Victorian chairs, several smaller rooms, and the *shosei* student's quarters. We ate in the central Japanese wing, where several large Japanese rooms on the ground floor could be joined together as needed. The rooms offered a sweeping view of the garden. At the back were the kitchen and the maids' quarters. Also on the ground floor was the huge Japanese bathroom, where Mama, Masa, and I bathed, the storage area, and the all-important telephone booth. The three of us and Fusa slept in three of the upstairs *tatami* rooms. The corridor to the right wing led to the "forbidden" and therefore most interesting part of the house. Grandpa and Grandma Tomii's private quarters were Japanese and were located downstairs. Upstairs, sixteen-year-old cousin Chiyoko had her Western-style rooms, where she kept her piano and many secret treasures. Chiyoko always locked her rooms.

I ran to the entrance upon hearing the gravelly sound of the rickshaw coming to fetch Grandpa. Beyond the entrance gates, I saw strangers on the street, the outside world. Mama, Tanabe-san the *shosei,* and the maids were already lined up to see Grandpa off. He often ran a fever and coughed, but if his temperature was under thirty-eight he'd go to lecture at the Tokyo Imperial University, and this was one of those mornings. Mama told me to be still, and that Grandpa was a great man, not because he was a Baron, but because he was a scholar and scholars needed quiet. By now, the rickshaw had been waiting twenty minutes. Grandpa came rushing out with Grandma behind him, and everyone helped bundle him up in his cloak, scarf, gloves, clogs, umbrella, and hat. He was then buried under blankets as he shouted, "Go as fast as you can, man, I'm late!" We all bowed to say goodbye, then Mama laughed. "When he gets to that steep hill, Grandpa gets two men to push from the rear, then he storms wildly into the classroom, waving his papers."

The scholar did a lot of reading all by himself. Undetected, I lurked outside his study, poking a hole in the paper of the sliding doors to watch him at his desk. He looked different from other people. With a white beard that trailed to the floor when sitting, he squatted at his desk, a white bandana tied around his head to help him concentrate. Although Grandma had slitty eyes and a flat nose, Grandpa had deep-set eyes and a high nose. Instead of sh-sh-ing like Grandma, he was always kind and courteous, though he never really seemed to see me; his mind was always somewhere else. When Grandpa was studying, he certainly did not see me, for nothing could distract him except my howls and kicks when a maid caught me peeking and tried to drag me away. Sliding open the paper doors, he looked amused and invited me in, until mother came running, apologizing and scolding.

I sometimes crept to the forbidden wing after bedtime. Mother's *futon* was still empty, and it was easy to crawl out from the room-sized green mosquito net. All *shoji* holes were immediately repapered, so I poked a new hole and watched Grandpa, bent over his desk, a candle lighting his calm face. (His room was the only place in the house where a candle was used.)

At times, he'd be in his sitting room, the doors left open. Grandma was often with him. I would often go to see them after tip-toeing away from boring grown-up talk. Once I stopped, after hearing my name being called. It was Grandpa.

"Shu seems to like his post in San Francisco. I can see Ayako becoming the apple of his eye."

Then Grandma: "His wife spoils the children. It's this foreign influence. All those years living in London and Berlin and Ottawa."

"Maybe because Shu isn't here right now."

"Masa's been hiding all his medicine under the rug in the parlour. The maids found a week's batch this morning."

Chuckles. "With a girl it doesn't matter, but a boy must have discipline, especially in Japan. I'll have a talk with him."

"Spoiled, spoiled, both of them are spoiled. Thank goodness they are leaving Masa in Japan."

Dinner was often a grand family affair. The sliding doors were removed between two ten-tatami mat rooms and tables were placed in a very long row. At the head sat Grandpa and Grandma, any guests present, as well as Masa, who always made faces. Family sat according to age and sex, Masa at the top as the eldest son's heir, then visiting uncles and boys. Mama headed the women, being the eldest son's wife, followed by aunts and girls. Chiyoko and I sat at the very bottom. Maids continually dashed back and forth.

This evening, Mama's youngest sister, Aunt Akiko, was visiting with Makoto, my favorite cousin, but he sat far away with the other boys.

"Had any letters from China, Aki-chan?" asked Mama.

"Yes, one yesterday. There seems to be fighting, but Ichiro doesn't go into details, just that he's well and thinking of us, hoping we bring up Makoto as an upright boy Japan can be proud of."

The Tachibanas were also visiting. Uncle Koichi worked in a large electrical firm; Aunt Sumiko was Grandpa's eldest daughter. One of their daughters, Kyoko, sat next to her favorite cousin, Chiyoko, her plainness contrasting with Chiyoko beauty.

"But Kyoko has brains," Mama always said. "And she has loving parents. Poor orphaned Chiyoko."

Aunt Akiko's voice rang above the others. "I don't know whether I like these prunes. After dinner, show me that washing machine and icebox Shu sent. How wonderful to have a husband in San Francisco instead of China, like my Ichiro."

Grandma snorted. "Don't be absurd. Ichiro is an officer fighting for his country. Besides, this washing machine is a waste of money. We have plenty of maids to do the washing. Hide, it is your job, after you get to San Francisco, to see that Shu becomes less spendthrift. Think of the soldiers protecting us in China. Washing machines and iceboxes indeed."

Cousins Chiyoko and Kyoko were chatting away near me. Forgetting to be aloof, Chiyoko was laughing. "Grandfather and Grandmother had a big fight this morning. You know how he likes to eat Roquefort at breakfast?"

"Oh yes, and does he still like to brew his own coffee? I always thought he looked like a magician, surrounded by his assorted jams, cheeses, and butter."

"Yes, but what I wanted to say was, he couldn't find his Roquefort and was looking all over for it, asking the maids and everything. And Grandmother saying not a word, with that deadpan look of hers. Finally, she says quite calmly, 'If it's that moldy cheese you're looking for, I buried it in the garden. Mold is bad for your health.' Grandfather gets up shouting, digs up the cheese, stares at the filthy thing, sighs, and says, 'What a waste, considering I ordered it especially from France with the wines.' Grandmother purses her lips and sniffs."

Gales of laughter.

"What's so funny, girls," Aunt Sumiko asks.

Giggles.

"They're enjoying themselves. Chiyoko rarely has friends over. Talking about school or clothes I suppose," said Mama.

Chiyoko continued, "Grandfather loves his food; he sometimes treats us at Seiyoken because he likes their French 'cuisine'—"

"Don't I know," Kyoko interrupted, "and he can be so embarrassing. There he's sitting, the sleeves of his woolen underwear showing under his kimono, eating all his bread before the courses come. Instead of asking for more, he looks around to see if anyone's watching, then he darts to the next table, snatches some bread and returns to his seat casting furtive glances all around. I could die."

Chiyoko laughed. "Grandmother says it's a leftover from his impoverished days at the University of Lyon. Says he came out from Kyoto, worked as valet to a French family on board ship to pay for his passage; then in Lyon he wore wooden clogs to save on shoes, sold books, and catalogued oriental art objects at the museum while he studied."

"Well, it must have been something to go all the way to France in those days, to come back and write the new Civil Code and become an advisor to the Emperor."

"Yes, he must like studying. Ugh."

"Talk about embarrassing. You know how he likes to hail a cab for us on the way back from the restaurant—"

"Oh, I know what you're going to say!"

"Well, we walk for a while, then as he sees a cab he dashes out to the middle of the street, waving his umbrella, shouting, "Five *rin* to Yakuohji," as if he were haggling. Naturally, the driver stops, first because he doesn't want to run over this bearded gentleman and second because five *rin* is double the fare for the distance. And when we get to the house in a matter of minutes, Grandfather throws open the door and dashes inside. The driver thinks maybe the gentleman has to rush to the bathroom. Instead, he whispers to Grandmother, who meets him at the entrance (you know how she never comes along because she can't stand 'the stench of butter'), 'How much should I tip?'"

"I wonder why he still takes a rickshaw to his classes."

I heard the phone ringing several times in the telephone booth. The maids were busy now, going back and forth from the kitchen. Presently, one of the maids came up to Grandpa.

"*Dannasama*, Master, Dr. Yamashita of the Tokyo Imperial University has asked that you call him back at his home after you finish dinner."

"Very well, I was thinking I must call him."

"He'll be in that booth forever," said Chiyoko. "Aunt Hideko said when Grandfather and her father used to talk over the phone, her father prepared himself by bringing in a brazier into his booth on cold days. It was hard not to forget the gist of the conversation, because Grandfather would talk in great detail in his scholarly way, and Aunt Hideko's father, being a businessman, liked to come to the point fast."

"Oh, was he a businessman?"

"Mainly so, didn't you know? Zeko Nakamura was head of the Manchurian Railways and also mayor of Tokyo. He was great friends with his classmate, the novelist Natsume Soseki. Uncle Shu says they commiserated with each other about nagging wives!"

Fusa appeared before me. "*Ojohsama*, it's bedtime. Say goodnight to everyone."

All of a sudden I felt very sleepy. How could calm Grandpa be so excitable? I remembered him rushing to his classes, but he still looked calm. Strange.

"Goodnight"

"Nighty-night"

"Goodnight."

Tag and hide-and-seek were not the only games we played in the rambling house. Favorite cousin Makoto came to play one afternoon with Masa. I was allowed to join them in a game of war, played with water pistols, because three would be more fun than two. I used an umbrella as a shield as we fought in the bathroom, but soon I was drenched, an easy target for Masa, who used his umbrella with more skill and remained dry.

"It's cowardly to shoot at your younger sister all the time."

"Bah!" Squirt, squirt in my face. "Yaay!"

"Here! I'll help you, Ayako," and soon it was two against one. We made such a ruckus that Mama routed us all with an ambush of maids.

"You'll all catch cold—and look at this mess!"

Makoto was eleven, just two years older than Masa, but oh, how different they were, Makoto wanting to become a soldier just like his colonel father. Boys weren't all nasty. I became his devoted slave.

Another rainy afternoon, Masa whispered, "Ayako, want to eat a lot of candy where nobody'll find out? Caramels and those chocolates Papa sent us?"

"Where, where? Show me."

Creeping upstairs to the *tatami* rooms in the central Japanese wing where we slept, Masa slid open a cupboard. There were futons piled at the bottom, then blankets, sheets, and pillows were placed on a sturdy shelf that divided the cupboard in half. It was dark inside.

"Here. I'll help you up."

I didn't want to go in, but was lifted onto the shelf.

"Look into the corner. No, the farthest one."

In a black corner, I felt a paper bag. It was full of caramels.

"You can start eating the caramels. I'll bring the chocolates."

I wailed.

"Won't take more than a minute. Be quiet or they'll find us. I'll leave the cupboard open. Eat a caramel." Masa disappeared.

I sat on a pillow near the cupboard door; our room looked strange and different from that height. Comforted by the warmth and quiet, I unwrapped a caramel. Inside, the caramel was wrapped in that transparent paper you could eat, and I let it melt on my tongue before I chewed.

Masa tiptoed up the stairs and clambered into the cupboard.

"Here." He opened a box of chocolates. We both munched. Yummy—lucky Papa, able to eat such chocolates every day. It was very cozy until Masa closed the cupboard door and it became pitch dark, except for a sliver of light at one end.

"It's scary!"

"Don't be stupid. They might find us; besides, it's more fun this way. Have some more chocolates."

I was not convinced, but continued munching, looking at the crack of light. "I dropped one! Oh! Here it is!"

"Sh-sh! I hear someone coming! Lie down in the far corner!" Masa closed the door tightly; now it was really dark. I felt the box of chocolates underneath my stomach as I lay down.

"I'm sure I saw *Obotchama* going up these steps a little while ago."

"Masa can take care of himself, but I haven't seen Ayako for some time, and I'm a little worried."

"*Okusama*, I haven't seen Miss all afternoon."

It was Mama and O-Kiku, the head maid of the house.

"Nobody here," came a cry from Fusa's room.

"Or here," from Masa's room.

"Or here," from close by.

"Strange."

"I'm sure I saw *Obotchama* coming up."

"Maybe he went downstairs again. He knows he's not supposed to come up here during the daytime."

I was beginning to feel sick, the caramels and chocolates taking their toll. "Masa, I want to get out!"

"Shhh!"

We heard cupboards opening and closing in Masa's room.

"Nobody here."

The footsteps were now nearby. I felt like crying.

"How about in here?" A crack of light appeared.

"Nobody."

"Wait." It was O-Kiku. "There's a strange smell. Like sweets. Her head became silhouetted against the opening door. "Why, they're both here, *Okusama*!"

"What?" Mama's head appeared and I threw myself at her.

"Why, look at this mess, *Okusama*! Chocolates all over the pillows!"

"You naughty children!"

"It was all Masa's fault!"

"Liar!"

"Look at this. Filthy, filthy. The pillows will have to be taken apart, washed and resewn!"

"Look at your clothes."

"I want to go to the bathroom."

"What will grandfather and grandmother say! And where did you get these chocolates? You're going to be punished, both of you!"

Grandma and all the maids had gathered before the uproar died down.

In 1950, Cousin Chiyoko led me to the site of the Yakuohji house. It was still intact, though dwarfed by the surrounding buildings. The gate was closed, but the gravel driveway was probably still there. Neighbors had sought haven there during the great Kanto earthquake of 1923. Chiyoko told me that in 1936, a few of the officers brought into Tokyo to quell the military coup of February 2nd were billeted in our Japanese wing. The house, which had seen so much history, had survived the air raids and fires of World War II.

Wedding picture of Shu Tomii and Hide Nakamura. January 14, 1923, Tokyo.

Hide Tomii dressed for her presentation to the Queen during Shu
Tomii's first posting in London 1924–1926.

Gathering of some members of the Tomii and Nakamura families. Hide Tomii (back, second from right), Baron Masaaki Tomii (front left), Baroness Masuyo Tomii(back,left), Zeco Nakamura (standing, second from right), Chiyo Nakamura (back, second from left). At the Nakamura home, now Hanezawa Garden, Shibuya, Tokyo. 1920's.

AMERICA

2622 Jackson Street

San Francisco meant reunion with Papa, now a tall, strong stranger who lifted me onto his shoulders with a mischievous smile. Papa and Mama were together a lot and smiled as if they shared a secret, as I came upon them. Papa soon became a friend, my best friend who smacked his lips at the pancakes I made on my toy cooker and asked for seconds, a friend who played hide-and-seek and knew such wonderful hiding places behind velvet curtains and in coat closets but never found me behind sofas or under beds. Games bored Mama.

I liked the house, as I was to like all the houses I lived in, for they were the homes where I could create my own special, private world. The house at 2622 Jackson Street, high up on Pacific Heights was large, like Grandpa's house, but so full of light and sunshine that just looking at it made me happy. The front lawn led up to a semicircle of columns that surrounded the entrance to the white stone house. It had three stories and a basement; I became intimate with the middle two floors, but the attic and the basement were off limits, and with no Masa to tempt me into adventures, I remained out of them. Downstairs, I was interested in the dining room, the breakfast room, the kitchen and cook Goto's room (which he kept locked). Upstairs, my interests took me to Papa and Mama's bedroom and its huge bed. Facing the front lawn, the room was filled with sunshine and had a bathroom that always smelled of flowers. Facing the back garden and the tangle of trees beyond were my bedroom, which I shared with Fusa, and to its left, my playroom. The other rooms were not part of my world, but the large staircase, with its curving banisters, was. The banister far from the wall was a joy to slide down. At first, Papa held me as I slid down the bottom quarter, then I climbed up by myself and managed the journey on my own, with Papa standing below. Mama would scold us, saying it was dangerous. She would have been horrified had she known that I sometimes slid right from the top when nobody was looking.

Evenings, tucked away in bed, Mama and Papa and their friends' laughter drifting up, I could hear the foghorns from the bay as the fog rolled in. Mornings,

I could see the bay from my bed, blue beyond the desk in front of the bay window.

The desk light still lit the room tonight, but it was dark outside. Fusa tiptoed in, closing the door, shutting out the sound of laughter. She looked at me as I pretended to sleep, then sat at the desk, opened a drawer and stared at the darkness. She started to write, top to bottom, top to bottom, her pen flew and tears rolled down her cheeks. I wondered. Fusa was always so cold, why was she crying and slipping pieces of green paper into an envelope with her letter? I sat up in bed.

"Why are you crying and what are you sending?"

Fusa jumped and turned, "You bad girl, why are you still up?"

"I was asleep, you woke me up."

"It's none of your business. I'm crying because you're such a bad girl."

"I'm going to tell Mama"

"Go ahead. I'm tired of all this."

Next morning, I cuddled between Papa and Mama in their double bed, warm and soft and comfortable and smelling so nice. On my right, hair tonicky Papa, on my left, Mama, perfume and flowers. "Can I sleep here at night, too?"

"No, you have your own room."

"But Fusa has her bed there, too. She was crying last night and putting pieces of green paper into an envelope."

"Oh dear." Mama knit her brows. "I wonder what's the matter. She's probably homesick, poor girl."

"Could be trouble back home. Sounds as if she's sending money."

"I'll have a talk with her. Her father begged me to bring her, so that she'd learn English and 'see the world,' but she's so sullen and doesn't want to learn anything. Doesn't mix with the Nisei maids, you know: Teruko and Hanako. Goto the cook, of course, doesn't talk to anyone except that dog of his."

"Well, anyway if she's remitting money, help her send a money order; it's risky to enclose cash. Poor girl, she's lonely. As for Goto, I've seen him flirting and chatting with Teruko, who speaks rather good Japanese."

"I've been wondering whether a Nisei maid wouldn't be better for Masako. She'll be going to kindergarten soon and should learn some English. You know, I'm rather afraid of Fusa myself."

"I didn't know you were afraid of anybody." Papa chucked Mama under the chin as he climbed out of bed. "Anyway, you do what you think is best."

A month later, Fusa returned to Japan, packing her suitcases in silence. Finally, she said, "Goodbye, I'm going home." She put her keys in her handbag.

I felt vaguely guilty. "Why do you have to go?"

"Because you're a bad girl."

I started to cry.

"Now, now, you're not really a bad girl, and you'll have Kimi, who'll take much better care of you than I did."

"Who's Kimi?"

"She's your new maid and she's a sweet Nisei girl. I'm going back because I miss Japan and because my father's ill."

"Goodbye. You'll come back?" Why did I say that if I'd never liked Fusa?

"Goodbye. Be a good girl."

Kimi did indeed turn out to be sweet. Sweet and insipid. Besides, I was now big enough to sleep alone in my room, so Kimi remained a distant, smiling figure. After some weeks, Kimi was with me mainly when I went out to the park or, later, to kindergarten and my piano lessons. The rest of the time she helped around the house and I was left to my own devices.

Friends

The back garden was my favorite playground, not the playroom lined with untouched dolls. Down the banisters and out to frolic with Spot, Goto's smooth-haired fox-terrier. Spot was a perky four-year-old that loved to dig in the flower-beds and to leap with joy at his master: three, four, five times with boundless energy. One command from him, however, and Spot would scurry into Goto's dark, tiny room. Spot tolerated me, but abandoned me at the hint of a whistle from his master, even if it meant being shut up in his room.

A huge palm-tree in the middle lent a tropical air to the garden. A circular flowerbed surrounded it and a circular lawn surrounded the flowerbed. The lawn sloped down to the surrounding concrete, where I rode my tricycle, round and round. To the left was the garage, entered by a separate driveway, and the chauf-feur's rooms upstairs, with flowered windowsills overlooking the garden. To the right were more flowerbeds, Spot's favorite burial spots for bones, and a small cherry tree that bore sweet dark cherries. Lattice hid the playground at the bot-tom of the garden. Not only was there a slide, swing, and warm sandbox, but there were also busy ants, worms, and snails that headed for the jungle of trees and bushes beyond a wire fence. If I cut a worm in half with my shovel, I would have two short worms that still crawled. It was both horrible and fascinating. If I poured salt on a snail, it melted. Who taught me that? Mama was indignant and wanted to know. Was it Goto? Was it Ikeda, the chauffeur? Bees and white and yellow butterflies mingled with the flowers. Sparrows were plentiful and some-times there would be a frog. Once, what appeared to be a worm the size of my arm burst from the jungle and I ran into the kitchen screaming.

"Probably a snake." Goto sounded nonplussed as he sipped coffee with Spot curled at his feet.

"But it was a worm; it was brown and had rings around it and it sprang up this high," I put my hand up to my neck, "and it had no eyes."

"A snake," Goto repeated without interest. He was usually morose or brusque, but he was always happy with Spot, and it piqued me that Spot preferred Goto to me. He was a mysterious being, dressed in white, surrounded by steaming pots ("Get out of my kitchen") or else disappearing behind a small door near the kitchen that led to his room. The door was always closed "to keep Spot in and from under my feet."

"That's where he drinks, *Okusama*," Fusa used to whisper to Mama. "That's why he can never get up in the morning and makes us maids cook breakfast."

"Can I see your room?" I asked Goto.

"No."

"Why not?"

"Little girls don't go into cooks' rooms."

One afternoon I was allowed into Goto's room. Mama and Papa were out, so I went into the kitchen for company. Kimi and the other maids seemed to be taking their afternoon rest, and only Goto was there, sipping coffee as usual with Spot at his feet. Instead of his surly self, he was in a rare good mood.

"You want to see something special?"

"Yes, what?"

"Promise you won't tell anyone."

"Promise."

Goto beckoned with his finger and entered his room. Hesitating for a minute, I looked around, then went in and was surprised and frightened at the small, dark, dirty room. "My, it's dirty."

"Shhh, quiet, or I won't show you anything." Then, quite unlike his arrogant self, he pointed shyly to his desk.

In the midst of candy-wraps, empty glasses, and broken toothpicks rose a castle made of sugar cubes: doors, windows, arches, and turrets, details from a fairy-tale book, all coaxed out of sugar. I was enchanted.

"See, it lights up." He switched on the little lights and the whole castle glowed. He smiled, his eyes soft—he looked quite nice without his frown.

"It's beautiful. It's the most beautiful thing I've ever seen."

"Well," he said, shrugging, "it's not finished yet. See, it needs a roof here and another tower there. There's still much more to be done."

"How could you have made this."

He looked annoyed. "It was a lot of work."

"Why did you make it?"

"Gives me pleasure. Besides, your father and mother have been good to me, and I want to give it to them as a Christmas present."

I clasped my hands and jumped up and down. "Oh, they'll love it. Aren't you nice."

"You like it, eh? It's pretty, isn't it."

I touched it lightly. "It's much nicer than my dolls. I wish I had it."

"Well, maybe they'll give it to you afterwards. Now, remember, don't you tell them. If you do, I'll tear down the whole castle."

"No, no, never. Promise."

There was a clatter of bottles and a soft thud. Spot had knocked over the beer bottles strewn on the floor and jumped onto Goto's soiled sheets. They were rumpled and half on the floor. I noticed a glossy picture pinned above the bed. It was very different from any I had seen: a beautiful lady with long hair and no clothes, strapped to a table and with two evil-looking men beside her. One had a lot of muscles and was cranking a circular saw. The other man was old and leering at the lady, who was half sawed through beneath her breasts.

"What a funny picture."

"Get away from there. It's not for little girls."

"Why isn't she screaming. Doesn't it hurt?"

"She's probably dead already. Now get out of here."

"Did you draw this picture? Who is it?"

"Of course I didn't. It's from a magazine. Now get out."

"Why do you have it up there?"

"Shut up. I should never have let you in." With that, I was pushed roughly out.

After that, Goto ignored me till Christmas. At Christmas, the fairy-tale castle, double the height now and ablaze with lights, appeared in the dining room. Papa, Mama, and all the maids gathered around to admire it.

"Come, Ayako, look. Isn't this wonderful. Goto made it."

Goto had be summoned and stood there looking sheepish and proud.

"I know, I saw it in his room. And I didn't tell, did I?"

"You went to his room?" Mama spoke sharply. Goto was smiling but looking uncomfortable.

"Yes, it was on his table and it was beautiful. Didn't tell, did I?"

Everyone was laughing and praising Goto.

Admired by all who came, the castle stood there till mid-January, when it was given to the Nippon Club so that more people could see Goto's masterpiece. But he was hurt that his castle had been given away; he had made it for our family and had wanted it to remain at Jackson Street. Mama sighed and said she had meant for the best—cooks were so temperamental.

One spring morning, as I watched a yellow butterfly in the garden, Goto, sobbing and choking, rushed in from the side gate with Spot in his arms. I was stunned, as this was the first time I had seen a grownup cry that way, like a child.

"What's the matter, Goto?"

He slammed the basement door without answering.

Dinner that evening consisted of stew and salad. I was staying up late and keeping Papa company as Mama was in bed with a cold.

"Simpler than Goto's usual fare, eh, Harada?" Harada, our butler, poured some more red wine for Papa.

"Kimi made dinner, sir. Spot got run over this morning and Goto's drinking again."

"Spot? The poor dog. How did it happen?"

"Well, sir, I saw it all, because I happened to be polishing the front doorknob. Goto was returning from the market, waiting for the traffic to thin before turning in to our driveway. Spot saw him from this side, dashed across the street, barking. "No, get back, Spot!" Goto shouted, but it was too late. Luckily, Spot was killed instantly."

"Why was Spot out front?"

Harada lowered his eyes. "He's never run out to the street before, sir."

"Goto was crying very loud, like a baby," I said.

"Poor Goto and poor Spot. They were inseparable."

When I played in the garden, I sometimes asked Ikeda the chauffeur to keep me company. Goto came from Japan, but Ikeda was a native Californian. Always smiling, he pushed my swing, ate cherries with me, and answered my questions. If Ikeda put the car in the garage while I was in the garden, I'd run up to him and ask him to play. If he didn't have to go out again soon, he'd laugh and keep me company for five or ten minutes before going up to his quarters above the garage. He'd wave to me when he watered his window-box flowers. He was tanned and had wavy hair.

"What's your place like? Can I see it?"

"Oh, it's quite nice. I have a complete set of rooms."

"Really? Goto's room is dark and dirty." I did not mention the picture.

"He has a bad room because he wants to be near the kitchen. Besides, he's a busy man."

"Aren't you busy?"

"Not as busy as he is. And driving isn't such hard work. I get out and see all sorts of places and people."

"Can I see your rooms?"

"Well, maybe some other time."

"Promise?"

"All right."

Ikeda kept his promise, and when I saw his place, I was very surprised. Overlooking our garden, everything was so pretty in the light and airy rooms: flounced armchairs, and in the bedroom, a neatly-made bed with a flounced bedspread and matching curtains at the windows. Loveliest of all, there were flowers everywhere, and not just in the window-boxes; there were pots of geraniums, begonias, and other blossoms I had never seen.

"What pretty rooms you have! But I thought only ladies had so many flowers."

"Everybody likes flowers." Ikeda went over to two canary cages that I had not noticed before because they were off in a corner of his living room. "Tweet, trrrrrrrrrrr trrrrrrrr, tweet, tweet."

"Make yourself comfortable. Would you like some orange juice?"

I was so impressed that I described Ikeda's canaries and flowers to Papa and Mama next morning when I jumped into their bed.

"Ikeda likes flowers just as much as passing other cars, eh?" Papa chuckled.

"I really don't like you going to the servants' rooms, Ayako. Ikeda shouldn't have invited you in."

"He didn't want to, but I asked him to, Mama."

"Still, he should have known better. I must have a word with him."

"Oh, please don't, please, or he'll never play with me again."

"He shouldn't anyway. You'll be going to kindergarten soon and you'll make plenty of friends there."

Mama became stricter. "She's not a baby any longer and needs some discipline."

Mama spanked me, Mama who had been gentle, beautiful, and smelled of perfume. Hearing my cries, Papa came and took my side.

"Don't hurt her."

"She's just pretending."

Papa and Mama argued, Mama shrill and Papa low and rasping. Usually, Papa and I won and Mama left in a huff, leaving me guilty and cowed. I was sorry I had been a bad girl, though I never said so.

Once, when I was especially bad, Mama locked me up in one of the attic rooms, for spanking had been abandoned. Screaming and kicking, I clung to the banister as I was carried to the attic and locked in a strange, dark room. Panic-stricken upon hearing Mama going down the stairs, I howled and kicked the door so hysterically that Kimi and then Papa came up and I was let out, vomiting and screaming.

"Don't get back at me through Ayako."

"You're a one to be finding fault. How about your own behavior, all your running around. What if I go away and never come back?"

Kimi had vanished and a great fight between Papa and Mama followed, with Mama in tears at the end and everyone feeling miserable.

"Don't go away, Mama. I'm sorry I was a bad girl."

"I'm not going away, I'm just tired. Come on, let's change you."

"We both love you very much."

It was shortly after this scene that Papa and Mama came to me, looking very grave.

"Ayako, Grandfather's very ill."

I thought of Grandpa with his white bandana, writing at his desk.

"Your father should go back, especially as he's the eldest son, but he can't because of his work. It would take weeks to go back and forth on the ship, so I'm going in his place. Do you want to come with your mother or stay with your father?"

I looked from Mama to Papa. "Why?"

"Your mother just told you, Grandfather is very ill and your mother is going back in my stead. We'd both like to have you with us, but you can't be in two places at once."

"Shu will spoil her dreadfully," Grandpa had said. I did not want to leave Papa or this house, with its sunny garden, but I wanted to be with Mama too.

"I want to stay here."

"It's only for a little while; your mother will be back soon."

Mama looked hurt. "Don't you like your mother?"

"Yes, but I like Papa better," I replied, clinging to his trousers.

"Of course you don't, but you want to keep your poor father company, don't you, or else he'll be all alone. Your mother will have Masa in Tokyo." Papa patted my head and repeated, "It'll only be for a little while; your mother will be back soon."

Mama's stateroom on the SS *Chichibu Maru* was full of flowers. Mr. and Mrs. Miyake came in, then Mr. and Mrs. Yoneda. Everyone was chatting, and I felt small and abandoned as I clung to Mama's skirts and looked straight ahead at waists. If I turned my head I could see baskets of flowers—the lavender ones were the prettiest, same as the ones Mama had on her lapel, with a pearl pin and a silver bow. Mama's hat was at a rakish angle with a little veil; she looked especially pretty.

Uu-uu-oo-oo-uuh! The *Chichibu Maru* gave a deep blast and Papa took my hand. "Have to start getting off. Thank you everybody for coming. Hide, take care of yourself. I leave Father in your care. My best to Mother and Masa. We'll be waiting for your return!"

"Be a good girl and listen to your father."

My throat felt funny. "I want to go with Mama! I like Mama after all!"

"Now, now, now." Mama was crying "I wish I weren't leaving."

"So do I," said Papa as he picked me up, tears, runny nose, and all. "Your mother will be back in no time. Keep your Papa company, won't you? We'll have good times together!"

The Miyakes and Yonedas made noises of sympathy.

Uu-uu-ooh-ooh-uuh! the *Chichibu Maru* slowly backed away from the pier, red, yellow, blue, orange, green paper streamers crisscrossing from its decks to the people waving on shore. "Auld Lang Syne" was played by the band on the pier. Mama had thrown many streamers to Papa and me and her friends, and she threw well, never wide of the mark. I was quiet, perched on Papa's shoulder, the better to see Mama. I clenched his eversharp pencil in my fists, looking at the five streamers he had stacked, twirling and twirling and becoming smaller and smaller, around the pencil.

Uu-uu-ooh-ooh-uuh!

The voices around me surged in volume: "Bon voyage!" "Good-bye!" "Hiroko, *genkidene*, take care of yourself!" "Come back soon; we'll be waiting for you!" "Write to us!" "*Gambatte*, do your best!"

The other end of my streamers were tied to the railing in front of Mama, who was unpinning her lavender flowers and shouting something to Papa. He put me down and lunged forward on the pier, bumping into people as he did so. The orchids flew through the air and landed on his outstretched palms, then bounced onto the concrete among smiles and whistles: "Golly, what gorgeous orchids." "Wish someone'd throw me a corsage like that." Papa brought me Mama's present.

"You dropped it!" I bawled.

"I could have caught it, but I didn't want to crush the petals, so I just broke the fall; it's better that way. Here, they were meant for you." Only one petal was slightly damaged, and Papa pinned the corsage on my dress amidst looks of admiration.

The pier seemed to be moving backwards as the streamers snapped and Mama waved and waved until she was only a dot among dots.

"Come on, it's time to go home. Let's take care of each other until Grandpa is better and Mama comes back." We were both in tears.

After Mama left, I was allowed to join Papa in the big dining room when there were no guests or when the guests were very close friends. Up till then, I usually ate with Kimi in a sunny alcove that faced our palm tree.

Dressed up by Kimi, I slid down the banister if nobody was looking ("You'll break a bone someday"), bowed to the guests and climbed onto my chair. Sometimes I curtsied, but that was only to Papa's many white friends, and I never dined with them. Mr. Miyake, Mr. Yoneda, Mr. Takahashi, Mr. Watanabe, Mr. Suzuki—those were familiar names.

"How she's grown." "Poor little thing misses her mother." "So well behaved." "You're lucky to have her here."

Soon they'd be engrossed in their talk and forget about me. Papa so loved to talk. I munched and watched the red glow of my goblet. I wanted to be served the same as everyone else, including the wine, and after much begging, a dash of red burgundy was mixed with my water in a crystal goblet, something that Mama never would have permitted. No matter that the water tasted bed, it was very pretty and made me feel important and grown up.

Papa was talking seriously. "The *Issei* first-generation delegation came again this morning."

"Good old Okumura?" Mr. Miyake helped himself to more asparagus.

"And Takei, Baba, and Miwa. They're so earnest and hard-working…such persistence in the face of so much prejudice, I wish I could help them more. Makes my blood boil to hear some of the things they have to put up with."

"You've helped a hell of a lot more than any of the other consuls we've had," Mr. Watanabe said.

"That may be true, but that's not nearly enough. These are difficult times and things could get even uglier. Darn it, I could do more if I were here longer. You have to persuade and convince the legislators that something should be done, and to do that you have to get to know them well, to earn their friendship and trust. Two or three years isn't enough to even scratch the surface, so it's up to people like you—educated, who live here, who understand both sides—to be more active."

"Ummm." Mr. Yoneda was masticating his sirloin. "But we lack your authority and nobody will listen to us."

"And of course, there's something in prejudice that legislation can't alter," Papa said before sipping his wine, "as my friend Doreen Spencer told me when I was young and green in New York: "'Shu, you rant about what's right and fair, that we should do this and we should do that, but I don't want to; it's a matter of feeling.' And with a shrug, she turned away from me. I thought, how true, feelings don't always follow reason."

"Maybe we should change our skin color."

"Watanabe with white skin and blue eyes? Making many blue-eyed friends would be more practical! America's a big country; there'll be place for Japanese Americans. Someday."

"That'll be in our grandchildren's generation. And the homeland certainly isn't improving our image lately."

"Ah, the militarists." Papa sat back and sighed. "No wonder the Jap image prevails. Oh well, let's put an end to such gloomy talk. When I retire, I'll live in San Francisco—I love California—and we'll organize, work together and play golf together." Goblets clinked. "Now it's off to bed with you, Ayako. Harada, ask Kimi to come and get her, will you?"

I sometimes accompanied Papa to baseball games in Berkeley, for he loved baseball, golf, tennis, billiards—any game using a ball.

"In my university days, my biggest dilemma was, 'Should I become a baseball player, a billiard player, or a diplomat?'"

I had no interest in baseball, but these outings were always festive occasions. I looked forward to them, for it was exciting to cross the bay on the ferry with Papa. The decks were thronged with holidaymakers who chattered in English, which I hadn't yet learned. I never mingled in such crowds except when Papa took me to see *Little Miss Marker,* starring Shirley Temple, and *Captain Blood,* with Errol Flynn. The people were very different from the guests at Jackson Street. Some were rough-looking, but all seemed to smile and eat and drink and be having a good time. Papa too, rakish in a cap and open shirt, just laughed at all the jostling.

"They say they're going to build a bridge here soon, all the way between San Francisco and Berkeley. Aren't Americans marvelous? You'll be able to see it from your window if we're still here then."

"We won't be able to ride the ferry to the ballgame!"

"The ferry ride and popcorn—that's what you like about baseball, hey?" He tossed some popcorn to a passing seagull.

"Can I have some more popcorn?"

Papa warmed up to the subject of baseball as we munched on a bench on the crowded deck. "I was a mean batter myself during student days. In fact, I was so fond of my bat that I slept with it beside my pillow, and that's how I earned a box of *manju*, you know, those Japanese cakes. You see, Grandpa made me become a *shosei*, sort of a glorified houseboy-tutor, for one year during university. He didn't want his eldest son to become spoiled, so he asked a very strict high school teacher to take me in. It was a Spartan household. I'd never been so hungry and cold in my life—you remember how Grandpa used to love good food and comfort. This was when I was mad about billiards as well as baseball, so I wasn't doing much studying. Well, one night as I was trying to sleep on a half-empty stomach, I heard funny noises. I opened my eyes to see a strange man heading for the door. He had pried loose the shutters on my windows. 'Stop!' I shouted, grabbing my bat and leaping from my bed. We stared at each other, me a skinny youth with little in his stomach and he, twice my size. I swung my bat menacingly. He silently slipped out the window. The next day, as a reward for my courage, the teacher's wife gave a box of six small *manju,* and no *foie gras* ever tasted better."

"How come you dropped Mama's flowers if you play baseball?"

Papa's face clouded. "That was on purpose, so as not to crush the petals. Wish your mother and brother were here with us now."

I missed Mama, too. Masa was remembered but was becoming a shadowy brother.

Mama never did return to San Francisco. Her two-week voyage included a stopover in Honolulu, To her, the gaiety there seemed out of place, as she hastened from her recent marital spats, to her dying father-in-law. Local boys swam out to the ship for tossed coins before it docked; hula dancers on the pier welcomed the passengers; the sun, clothes, and flowers were even brighter than San Francisco's. Papa read me one of Mama's letters from Tokyo, which arrived after the telegram that said Grandpa had died.

> As you already know, I was not in time to tell your father how wrenching it was for you not to be able to come in person to say farewell. It was only a difference of a few days, and I keep on thinking of the 'if onlys.' If only the ship could have been a little faster, if only there had been an earlier ship, if only your father could have held on for a few more days…but it's no use thinking like that. At least I was in time for the funeral, where so many mourners came to pay tribute. He was a man of character and a loving family man. Masa carried himself with dignity as heir in your absence as the head of the bereaved. I was told that when the Emperor's envoy arrived bearing tokens of condolences right after your father's death, Masa received the honors with admirable protocol. A diplomat's son indeed.

One of your father's colds developed into pneumonia. As you know, his lungs were not the strongest and he was getting on in years. According to those who nursed him, he was calm and gentle as usual and did not suffer too much. But your mother said that though he never complained, his eyes seemed to be searching for you, and he always asked about you when Masa dutifully came. Masa seemed ill at ease and left as soon as he decently could.

"Doesn't Grandpa ask about me?"

"He's fond of you, but you're a girl and won't be carrying the family name. That made a difference to Grandpa." Papa continued reading:

> I was touched to hear from Chiyoko that several neighboring townspeople kept vigil in our driveway during your father's illness and that former *shosei* and students seemed to be here all the time.
>
> The electric ice-box I brought from you to your father was not in time for him to benefit from it, but it is causing much wonder and giving much-needed joy in these sad days. Your mother says little, but this is a difficult time for her. She is often short with me. I seem to get on her nerves and I don't blame her. I have become "Americanized" and "spoiled" without knowing it. Tokyo seems so changed now, or maybe I have changed. You see a lot of uniforms—soldiers and policemen—and most of them are quite arrogant. They are serving their country, so we should be grateful, but you are serving your country, too. The way Aki-chan talks, you'd think her husband (now a general) is a model patriot and you a dilettante. I try to keep my mouth shut, but as you know, that is very difficult. I miss you and Ayako, though it's good to be with Masa, who needs some parenting…

When the telegram came saying Grandpa had died, Papa's face frightened me. Lots of people went in and out. A week later, Mr. Yoneda stayed for dinner.

"A great man. What a loss, not just for you and the family, but for Japan. Where will he be buried?"

"At Gokokuji Temple in Tokyo, though the Tomiis up till now have been buried at Shinnyodo Temple in Kyoto."

"Were they scholars like your father?"

"I really don't know, though we do have a scroll that traces the genealogy back to Genji. How reliable it is once you go back several hundred years is anybody's guess. What's for sure is that grandfather Masatsune Tomii, whom I never knew, was a samurai in the service of Prince Kitashirakawa and was dispatched to the Emperor to manage the imperial finances. After changes in political fortunes, Masatsune started a *terakoya* one-teacher school in Kyoto, which my father attended before going to Lyon."

"It would be interesting to find out more about your ancestors some day. Isn't Shinnyodo where Murasaki Shikibu of *The Tale of Genji* fame is buried?"

"Said to be, but as I said, we really can't visit the grave as often as we'd like to if it's in Kyoto. After a generation or two, it'll be even more abandoned, and if there's nobody to care for the grave, you know that you have to give back the plot to the temple."

"So, you give back the plot and the priests sell it again to somebody else at an exorbitant price?"

"I wouldn't put it quite that way. I will take care of all our ancestors' graves at Shinnyodo, and I'll tell Masa to do the same, but I don't know what will happen after that. Anyway, my mother seems to be quite happy with Gokokuji and is having her name engraved besides my father's."

"But she's not dead yet!"

"You've been away too long. Many women still do it, with a veneer of red paint on their names, to be washed off when they actually do die. No merry widows for them."

Papa regained a little of the twinkle in his eyes.

In the upstairs sitting room, an altar was decorated with white flowers, incense, and a big photograph with a black and white ribbons on the top corners. There was Grandpa, kimonoed, underwear slightly showing at the wrists of his kimono sleeves, white bandana (specially discarded for the picture) on his lap. He stared at me with his gentle eyes and looked very familiar. I was made to go every day to the altar with Papa to burn incense, hit the little gong, bow to the photo, and pray.

Ping, ping, ping. Hitting the gong with the wooden stick was fun, but the rest was boring. It was so gloomy, I amused myself by admiring a paper dove perched to the left of the photograph. It was made of white paper and something silvery and was more beautiful than any real dove.

"Papa, can I have that bird?"

"But that's Grandpa's."

"He wouldn't mind my putting it in my playroom?"

"Well, if you like it so much, maybe later."

"Oh, Papa, thank you. It's beautiful. I wish Grandpa would die every day."

Papa looked grave. "You shouldn't say such a thing. He was my father, and I couldn't go to him when he was dying and asking for me."

I looked puzzled.

"Oh well, I suppose you're too small to understand."

Papa had been busy lately and I did not see him too much. Groups of *Issei* came, talking in serious voices and continuing to talk at dinner time, and I was eating again with Kimi in our alcove. Americans came too, but they laughed more.

On one of the now-rare days that Papa came to my playroom, he was excited and in a good mood.

"Look at these." He showed me three handkerchiefs, one pink, one yellow, and one blue, and a pair of ladies' stockings. They felt soft, like silk, but more slippery, and the handkerchiefs were like thick lace. "This is rayon; isn't it amazing, these new American inventions. It's going to be used a lot in the future, you wait and see. The silk industry will suffer, though. You keep the handkerchiefs, I'm going to send these stockings to your mother."

Kindergarten

One Saturday, I was called into the drawing room at tea-time and found Papa laughing with Mrs. Miyake and two pretty American ladies.

"Ayako, the ladies are reminding me that you should be going to kindergarten and learning English."

"I don't want to go to kindergarten."

Laughter. Mrs. Miyake bent down. "You're all by yourself at home. At kindergarten you'll make lots of friends."

"Don't want any friends. I have Papa and Ikeda and Goto and Kimi."

More laughter. "You must really have spoiled her, Baron Tomii." After Grandpa died, Papa was called "Baron Tomii" and Mama "Baroness Tomii" by Americans. "Another reason why kindergarten would be good for her." Papa turned to the American lady:

"Isn't there a school two blocks to the right as you go out our front door?"

"But that's a Catholic one, and you wouldn't want your daughter indoctrinated in a Catholic kindergarten."

"Oh, do they indoctrinate children? I didn't know that. Where would you suggest?"

"You wouldn't want to send your child to that kindergarten unless you were a Catholic yourself. There's a public school four blocks to the left, down the other way, and it has a kindergarten section. I think sending her to public school would be the best way for her to learn the American way of life."

"Maybe you're right. And it's within walking distance, too," said Papa.

I pouted and ignored the ladies' smiles.

And so began my life at the kindergarten attached to Public School 8. It was clean and impersonal. I had never seen so many children at once, lively ones who did not defer to me. Instead of being the leader as I had been with my few Japanese friends, I was now shy and often left out. I spoke no English and understood only a little.

"At her age she'll pick it up in no time." "It's the best and most natural way, with friends." "She'll be a little American girl before you know it."

35

Indoor "classes" were a blank, but little was expected anyway. Occasionally, storybook time would stir my interest (provided the books had lots of pictures), but more often I sat apart and watched the other children. Most had white skin, there were none like me, and a few had very black skin. It was the first time I had been close to people with such dark skin, wide noses, and frizzy hair; they were so lively, jumping around twice as much as the other children. They kept mostly to themselves except when the teacher called on everyone to join together in a game. I was fascinated and afraid.

It was outdoors that things happened. There was a large concrete playground with grilled fencing that kept out two busy streets. There were swings and slides in one corner, but mostly the playground was bare so that we could run around and play games. Benches lined the walls of the building and there was a quiet place around one corner. As I slunk against one wall, a child, often a black child, would beckon me to join and play. Language did not matter in tag and by the end of playtime I'd be laughing with the others and we'd go indoors together, the best of friends. "Oranges and Lemons" I didn't understand well and was clumsy; the others made faces and told me to go away. I was often the butt of practical jokes.

One morning, two black girls, Emma and Susan, came to me in the courtyard, all smiles. They were especially nice and we sat on a bench in the quiet area, away from the others. Emma and Susan chatted together, smiled, then put some candy in my pockets. I smiled back, grateful for this sign of friendship. Emma pointed to something on the other side of the playground:

"Look! Look!"

I looked but saw nothing special. I looked around upon hearing peals of laughter and I saw my friends sticking their tongues out and waving the candies that should still have been in my pockets.

"Yellow, yellow, you're a yellow Jap!"

I felt in my pockets and the candy was gone.

Another morning, Emma and Susan blindfolded me, saying we were going to play hide and seek, then abandoned me in a corner while they ran to play on the swings. When I removed the blindfold at long last I heard,

"Ya-ay, stupid Jap. Dirty Jap." They stuck out their tongues as they said this.

"Niggers!" shouted a boy

"Jap, Jap!"

"C'mon, I'll play with you. I'm Billy." He took me by the hand just as we had to go indoors.

Yet, taunts and all, I enjoyed my time outdoors. There were so many new games that I could play there that I could not play by myself at home.

In the evening I asked Papa, "What's 'Jap'?"

"Where did you hear that word?"

"Emma and Susan called me 'Jap.' They wouldn't let me play with them."

"Well it means you're Japanese. Papa's Japanese and so are Mama and Masa. It means you come from Japan. Except that 'Jap' is not a very nice word. It means you look different."

"It's the niggers who call me that."

"Now, where did you learn the word 'nigger'?"

"That's what Billy calls Emma and Susan. And some of the other children, too."

"That's why Emma and Susan call you 'Jap.' They're called 'nigger,' a bad word, because of their 'black' skin, so they call you 'Jap,' another bad word, because of your 'yellow' skin. Anyway, stay away from those mean girls; there must be plenty of other children to play with."

I did not understand. In my room I looked at myself in the mirror. I knew what "yellow" meant—I understood more English words now—and yes, I had yellow skin and slanting eyes and straight black hair. I wish I had white skin and blue eyes and curly yellow hair like this doll, I thought, hugging a hitherto despised Shirley Temple doll. I took a pair of scissors and snipped off all of Shirley's curls.

Billy, meanwhile, was bothering me in a different way. Ever since he'd come to my rescue, he'd butt in as I played with other girls; he'd make faces and try to join in until chased away.

He was also distracting indoors. Now that I understood more English, I really enjoyed storybook time. I sat at the back, still shy, looked at the pictures, listened, and tried hard to understand. Billy, who hated storybook time, crept up to me, poked me in the ribs, and opened his fist to reveal a dead frog. I jumped up, knocking over two girls.

"Ayako, sit down and behave yourself."

I tried unsuccessfully to explain that it was all Billy's fault, that he had a dead frog. Billy shrugged his shoulders and feigned innocence.

"Don't give excuses; you're holding up the story. Go and stand in the corridor; and Billy, you go too."

Sorry to miss the end of the story, I went out, followed by a laughing Billy. He offered me gum from his pocket (Was the frog in there?), which I haughtily refused. I hated boys.

My kindergarten days came to an ignominious end after three months. We were trying to line up inside, waiting to be dismissed.

"Where's my sweater?"

"I can't find my book."

"Miss Drake, Johnny pushed me!"

"You pushed me first!"

"When can we go, Miss Drake?"

"Ouch!"

I wanted to go to the bathroom badly, so I pushed my way to the front and tugged at a harassed Miss Drake's sleeve. She paid me no attention. Another tug.

"Miss Drake."

"What do you want?"

"*Oshii-shi.*"

"What?"

"*Oshii-shi.*" Oh, what was the word for pee-pee in English? I started to run.

"Come back here!"

"*Oshii-shi.*"

"I said get back here."

I could wait no longer and peed into my pants and onto the floor, making quite a big puddle. A clearing opened around me, and there were giggles. Billy was holding his nose.

"Ooh, it stinks."

Miss Drake was cross. "Oh, Ayako you naughty girl, go to the bathroom. Why didn't you say you wanted to go?"

I hung my head and burst into tears as I ran.

The next day I didn't want to go back to kindergarten, and besides, I was feeling funny. I had come down with chicken pox, and after the first bad days it was rather pleasant to be lying in my bedroom with its view of the bay or lolling about in my sunny playroom. I was the center of attention of Papa and the household.

"You don't have to go back to kindergarten if you don't want to, my poor little girl."

I felt deliciously sorry for myself.

Piano Lessons

Now that I no longer went to kindergarten, Mrs. Spencer persuaded Papa to send me to a piano teacher.

"I know an excellent lady, retired from the Carmody Music School, where she taught for years and years, and you know, Baron Tomii, she lives only three blocks from here, near the park. It would be nice for your daughter to have a ladylike accomplishment, especially without her mother here."

Kimi took me once a week to Mrs. David's, left me there, and came to fetch me an hour later. I quite enjoyed the walk to and from Mrs. David's, to the right of the park across our street, then left past rows of cheerful small houses. I would occasionally see a boy roller-skating on the pavement or girls laughing, arm in arm. Once I ran into two kindergarten friends.

"Ayako, why don't you come anymore?"

"Chicken pox."

"Well, you don't have it now, do you?"

I mumbled and cast my eyes downward.

"Aren't you silly. Want to play with us in the park?"

Kimi explained that I was going to my piano lesson.

Mrs. David's house was like all the others: small and with lots of flowers in front. Her drawing room was small, too, and overflowing with things. A big, black grand piano took up half the room; the other half was crowded with dark, stuffed armchairs, dark little tables, and lots of aging lace.

Mrs. David herself had grayish eyes, grayish hair, and grayish clothes. She was the oldest person I had ever seen except for Grandpa and Grandma, and well, they were Grandpa and Grandma, so that was different. But when Mrs. David smiled, and that was quite often, she looked quite young. She had the nicest smile I had ever seen, including Mama's, although not Papa's.

"Let's play this." Mrs. David tinkled the lower keys of the piano and I would imitate her an octave higher till I had it right.

"Ve-ery good." Mrs. David smiled with surprise and delight and I felt very proud. She brought out a notebook and drew. "This is what those sounds look like—little twirls." We drew those twirls together, then I colored them. It was fun.

"You've been a very good girl." Mrs. David brought out a box of Turkish delights and said, "Choose one."

The jellies were jewel-colored and covered with powdered sugar. I took a ruby one. Mrs. David popped an emerald one into her mouth. "My favorite sweets. Don't you think they're good? Now, you let me play and you dance to the music."

It was very difficult to turn and skip without crashing into armchairs and tables, but I managed a few hops.

"That was very pretty. Now move your arms, too; listen to the music well and you'll look like a fairy."

I windmilled around, finishing with two sliding steps and bumping my knees against an armchair. I liked moving around after all that sitting, and I did not feel silly. I was a fairy.

"Wonderful. So graceful. Now, shall we play that first tune again? Do you remember it?"

"Can I have another Turkish delight first? The yellow one?"

I did quite well with my piano lessons and soon it was time for my first recital.

"It's just a little recital for the parents here in my house, but it gives the children something to work for."

"But she can't play anything yet."

"You'd be surprised. She has a great sense of rhythm."

A four-year-old boy played "Jack and Jill" to enthusiastic applause by parents and grandparents. Then it was my turn, a very simplified version of "The Maiden's Prayer." I curtsied and started playing. A mistake, then another. What did it matter? Mrs. David had said to play as usual, and I always made mistakes. A big fly started to buzz around and landed on a piano key. *Bzz-zz-zz-NYA-bzzz.* A fly shouldn't be there. *WHAM.* With good aim I squashed the fly, producing a discordant sound. I wiped my hand on my white dress and continued playing while roars of laughter came from the audience. Surprised, I looked up to faces of smiling approval.

"Go on, go on dear," my father said, then he turned and commented to another audience member, "She's so natural."

I enjoyed the piano lessons. Although I loved our house and garden, the three blocks to Mrs. David's were a change, and I was becoming curious about the outside world. I even missed kindergarten, although I'd insist to a sympathetic Papa that I hated it and didn't want to go back.

"Anyway, we'll be returning to Japan soon and we'll see Mama and Masa again."

"What does Mama say?"

"You know, I have a letter here that just came from her. Let's see what she says." Papa opened the letter and read:

> The cherry blossoms have been in bloom for only three days, but heavy rain and wind have already scattered the pink blossoms all over the garden. I wish you could have been here when they were in full bloom.
>
> You would have been a such a pillar of strength, too, during the events of recent weeks. A man is needed in the household.
>
> Your younger brother Yujiro and his wife came to stay, as you suggested. Even Yujiro was better than no man, or should I not be so impertinent. Well, you know how refined and aloof he is, like a prince, not liking to be embroiled in family arguments for fear he might tire and take ill (of course, he is rather frail). I knew he was a stickler for cleanliness, but never realized how much till he came to live with us. Do you know that if anybody sits in his favorite rattan chair, he'll take out his cotton-wool container (similar to a hip flask), pull out alcohol-soaked wads, and sterilize the chair before sitting down! Masa, wicked boy, often sits there on purpose in his school uniform, impregnated with outdoor germs. Yujiro has a special closet for his coats and suits worn outdoors, where germs are rampant.
>
> It's really your youngest brother, Takeo, who causes problems. You remember you were so happy he had settled down, your little playboy brother, with the ideal girl for him: of good family, pretty, and very understanding of his Bohemian ways. Well, it seems she is too understanding, and they both carouse together. Your father used to pay Takeo's debts, but you know how upright and stubborn your mother is. She refuses to help him, so he has touched several friends of your father for money. It is very embarrassing. Two nights ago he barged in drunk, saying he was going to join the army because everyone treated him like a leper, that it was the family's patriotic duty to pay off his debts, that you were living in luxury, playing golf and going to parties while he was going off to die for his country. I was quite frightened at his roughness. I must say for your stubborn mother, that she's much more courageous than I am. She sat there in the drawing room with that impassive Buddha look of hers and refused to give in to his demands. Takeo said his wife had pawned all her jewels but that they were still neck deep in debt. He started to shout, and your quiet mother shouted right back at him, still without batting an eyelash. The maids were eavesdropping, cowering behind the doors. He brought his face near your mother's and shook his fists. I thought he was going to hit her, so I grabbed his arms, but he flung me away (I almost hit my

head against the wall), then he smashed the teacups, scooped up the large Sèvres vase so treasured by your father, and said, 'I'll take this' and stomped out of the house. It was terrible...

Why, Ayako, I'd forgotten I was reading this letter to you. Not very suitable for young ears, I'm afraid."

The Park

I now wanted to play, not with the docile daughters of Mama's friends, but with lively children like the ones at kindergarten. That is not to say that I wanted to go back there, however. Anyway, Papa said we'd be returning to Japan soon to Mama.

I was allowed to go to the large park in front of our house, where there was a playground down at the other end.

Both Kimi and I enjoyed these outings to the playground very much. We'd go in the afternoon, when there were lots of children, and Kimi would sit on one of the benches under the trees and chat with the mothers. There were swings ("Higher, higher!"), seesaws, a huge slide, and hedges along one side of the playground. The slide was five times the height of ours and had two humps in the middle; if you had the knack, you could whiz down till the middle, then brake between the humps by spreading your legs and grabbing the sides. Your palms hurt, but the fun was worth it. As for the hedges, there were two, side by side. One faced the playground, the other faced a concrete path, and the narrow space between the hedges formed a tunnel. You went in from one end and there were side tunnels and holes from which you could crawl out before reaching the other end. It was dark and secret there.

"Come and play, Ayako."

"Let's play hide and seek."

"You're It"

"Ooh, do you live in that big house across the street at the other end? I'd like to live in a house like that. Can I come and play?"

Kimi said no, you did not bring strangers home.

One day, Billy appeared at the playground, and much to my annoyance he started coming regularly. But now I could talk back to him.

I was having a tea party in a sub-tunnel with two other girls when a freckled-face peered in.

"Can I come too?"

"No you can't; boys don't drink tea."

"I can too drink tea." Billy crouched besides us, cocked his little finger, and drank an imaginary cup of tea. "Umm-mm, it's good, can I have some more? With sugar?"

"Go away!" I pushed him, but he didn't budge. All three of us attacked him and he fell back laughing.

I was waiting at the slide one day (a slow business that afternoon because it was crowded) when a little boy climbed to the top, only to be afraid to come down till an older girl slid down with him. Another boy climbed to the top and remained there on purpose, sticking his tongue out and making the others wait until he was jostled down. At last it was my turn and I prepared to swoosh down. Billy clambered up from the bottom of the slide and lodged himself between the humps.

"Get away!"

Billy looked back at me, laughed, and shook his head. I'd show him. I'd knock him down with my feet. Down I slid to the first hump, my shoes hitting his back, which held firm. Another boy was climbing up. To pull Billy's legs? I couldn't wait. This wasn't so high, and I'd jumped before, so over the side I jumped.

"Ouch." I landed rather badly on my left shoulder but shook off Kimi's helping hands.

"Let's go home now. You can have juice and cookies."

I didn't object, as I'd had enough for one afternoon. "Don't tell Papa that I jumped."

"That was very dangerous."

"I won't do it again, ever, if you won't tell."

"All right, but that's a promise"

"I promise."

By the next morning, one shoulder was higher than the other and the pain in my left one was unbearable. "Don't tell Papa or he won't let me go to the playground anymore."

"But I must tell your father. I should have told him yesterday."

"Please don't, please."

X-rays showed a broken collar bone, and I was in a cast for a month. By the time the cast came off, our move back to Japan and Mama had been set. I did go back to the park once, though, because Papa said I could invite my friends over to play before we left. They did get to see the house, and I was able to say a proper goodbye to my American friends. From Japan, in a few months, I was going with Papa and Mama to a place called London.

   In 1994, when I was in San Francisco for a few days, I revisited 2622 Jackson Street. The house was still there, a little grayer, but otherwise the same from outside. The front lawn was also as I remembered it. I walked around to the back, as the kitchen driveway was gateless now, and found that the garage and Ikeda's quarters had been converted into a gallery. A house had been built on my playground beyond the back fence and probably more houses in the jungle behind the playground. The garden itself had become a concrete courtyard with no lawn, flowerbeds, or trees to obstruct the parking cars. After a few minutes' hesitation, I rang the side bell, not daring to go to the front. There were four different buttons (Was the house now split into apartments?) and I rang all of them, receiving no response. Partly relieved—for what would I have said, that I had lived there more than fifty years ago and could I see a little of the inside?—I went to the gallery where a smiling young lady welcomed me to a room full of contemporary art. We struck up a conversation and this very kind dealer told me that 2622 Jackson Street had been the Red Cross headquarters and then a music school. Recently, it had been bought by Agnes Bourne, an interior decorator, and her husband and that San Francisco's annual decorator showcase had been held there. The house, designed by Willis Polk in 1894, was a historic and protected building, as it was the first stone house to be built in San Francisco. So saying, she presented me with two prints made for the centenary of the sandstone house. Ms. Bourne was away at the moment, which was a shame, but if I wanted an inkling of what the inside was like now, I should look out for the "Before and After" section of the February 1995 issue of *Architectural Digest*. For the "showcase" exhibit a few months ago, famous decorators had completely remodeled the house, which had hardly been touched before and badly needed modernizing. (I have that issue, but there are no echoes of the past in those "before" rooms, which were stripped bare, with just vacuum cleaners and paint pots littering the floor. The redecorated rooms comprise a new house entirely).
   I thanked the kind gallery owner, knowing Ikeda would have been happy that his territory had turned into such a welcoming place for me. I took snapshots and then wandered to the park across the street. Strange that it should seem so much larger than I remembered—I had thought memories shrank in size as one grew bigger. Perhaps the whole park was centered in the playground, for a child. The park was big and very bare; gone were the hedges around the playground, and few trees had survived. It remained a welcome piece of open space, however, in the now-built-up Pacific Palisades.

Baron Shu Tomii, a nurse, Ayako. In front of 2622 Jackson Street, Pacific Heights, San Francisco, 1934.

Ayako and Spot. Under the palm tree in the garden. 2622 Jackson Street, 1934.

Ayako. In front of 2622 Jackson Street. 1935.

ENGLAND

The Voyage and the House on Bayswater Road

It was 1936. Papa had gone first again, by ship through Suez to Marseille, from there by train to Calais, then on to his new post as 1st counselor in London. The months in Japan had been a flurry of reunions and packing. Mama and I, with the maid Hana, sailed three months later on a voyage that began with frequent life-boat drills. Sometimes I'd wish the ship would sink so that I could show off how quickly I could put on my life-jacket, run to my station on A-deck, and jump into my boat, though I'd never done that part yet.

Soon I discovered shipboard pleasures. After all, we were to be on board for two months (or was it three months?) with all the ports of call, and we had to be kept happy.

It was a good idea to be on deck around 10:00 A.M. That was when a steward walked up and down the deck in his white jacket, alerting passengers on his xylophone-like instrument that they would be fortified with beef broth. With the bracing sea air, no ice-cream tasted better than this 10:00 A.M. consommé.

There was deck golf and ping-pong and costume parties. For *sukiyaki* parties, the A-deck was covered with straw mat *tatamis*, the portholes and walls camouflaged with red and white striped awning. We sat on cushions at low tables, and to make the Japanese setting complete, the purser and younger officers wore *geisha* costumes, complete with wigs and rouge.

The stopovers provided a welcome change. I remember the apple-green snakes of Penang slithering throughout the temple, on the floors, walls, and ceiling. Would one drop on my head with a plomp? I had never seen Mama so afraid.

"Snakes are what I most hate in the world."

The guide picked one up. "They won't bite, madam."

If Penang remained vivid partly because of Mama's intense fear, Suez remained so because of her laughter and excitement.

"I'm going to see the pyramids, Ayako, and ride on a camel! I'll tell you all about it afterwards."

"I want to go too."

51

"The next time, dear. You're too small yet; I wouldn't want you falling off a camel. I'll bring you a nice present. Now, Hana, remember, close the portholes and lock the door. This is a very dangerous place."

I pricked up my ears at "dangerous." I would be missing a lot of fun, so I hoped Mama's present was a large enough one to make up for what I would be missing. The day was long, hot, and quiet. It was as if everyone had abandoned me, except Hana. Mama was really coming back, wasn't she?

It was already evening when Mama returned with her friends, her eyes sparkling.

"Have you been a good girl? See what I brought you. Maybe it's too nice for a little child!"

I fingered the silver filigree bracelet. It was like wide silver lace and different from any of Mama's, it was a fairytale bracelet.

"Ayako, I rode a camel at the pyramids, a real camel. I thought it would be so easy with my horseback riding, but ooooh, that horrible feeling as the camel stood up! I thought my stomach would turn over!"

Marseilles was fittingly a gustatory adventure. A Mr. Tanaka took Mama, Hana and me to a seafood restaurant in a noisy, smelly seafront quarter, crowded with fishing boats and excited people milling around. Mr. Tanaka himself was more excitable than most of the Japanese gentlemen I was used to seeing.

"This is the best place for sea urchins! See, this fellow's opening sea urchins right here at the foot of the entrance steps—it's our Japanese *uni,* called *oursin* here!" A burly man was dipping his hands into a bucketful of porcupine-like balls and cracking them open on a chopping board. Something orange oozed. The man offered opened *oursins* to Mama with a spoon that he wiped on his apron.

"Eat them, they're absolutely delicious!" urged Mr. Tanaka.

Mama backed away a few steps. "No, thank you. I think I'll wait till we go inside."

"No?! You don't know what you're missing!" Mr. Tanaka slurped the *oursin* into his mouth with the spoon, then rolled his eyes. "*Délicieux!*"

Inside, we did have *oursin,* the specialty of the house, at Mr. Tanaka's insistence.

"Is it safe?"

"Safe?! It's fresher than what you get in Tokyo! Spread it on bread, that's what everyone does here."

"Bread! How revolting!"

"No more than eating it with rice." Mr. Tanaka spread a generous helping of *oursin* on bread and woofed it down. "Mmm...*délicieux! Merveilleux!*"

We imitated him tentatively. It *was* delicious with a smooth, rich flavor.

"It *is* good" Mama sounded surprised. "Can I have some more?"

Papa was waiting for us at Southampton, smiling and handsome.

"My two girls! I thought you'd never come. That voyage took years. Should have taken the train from Marseilles."

"Yes, it was a long voyage, but trains are so much more tiring than ships. I must say you look well, too, well for my liking; you must have been splendidly looked after!.."

"Now, now, that's all thanks to Ada. She used to work for the manager of the Yokohama Specie Bank and he recommended her highly, so I persuaded her to come and be our cook-general."

"What's a cook-general?"

"That's someone who cooks and also helps with the general housework. She's very good-natured and willing; says she loves Japanese people and working for Japanese. That attitude in itself is a jewel in 1936 London, with anti-Japanese sentiment running high." Papa pursed his lips.

"You said that you found us a house?"

"Yes, I hope you like it. I wasn't keen on the location on Bayswater Road, but the house has central heating—it used to belong to an American. That's what made me take it. There's nothing I hate more than a damp, cold house during a London winter. You remember when we lived here—when was it—from 1924–27?"

"Yes, that's when Masa was born. San Francisco's spoiled you."

"Weatherwise, yes. Although I must admit, our house at St. Petersburgh Place was rather lovely, so easy to walk over to Kensington Gardens with Masa…those were the years of pro-Japanese sentiment, too. Our old friends still remain true, though; they have been most decent; you can see why so many of us became Anglophiles."

"And St. Petersburgh Place will always be special, because Masa was born there. By the time I had Ayako in Berlin four years later, I went to a hospital for the birth."

I found the house dark and old, so different from sunny Jackson Street and the open rooms of Yakuohji. It scared me.

"See, there's a grand piano here in the drawing room for Ayako and the garden has all sorts of berries: blackberries, gooseberries, elderberries—"

"Raspberries?"

"No raspberries, I'm waiting for you and Mama to grow them!"

I tried to picture Mama planting raspberries but couldn't. The drawing room was a larger, finer version of Mrs. David's. In the garden, which was surrounded by brick walls, a lawn as smooth as water greeted the eye, with stripes flowing back and forth. At the back were tangles of bushes—this must be where the berries grew. No flowers brightened the garden at this time of year, and beyond the walls I could see the backs of three buildings. It was damp and cold and we were glad to return inside to see the upstairs.

"This is our bedroom. See how large it is, with a sitting-room area almost as large as the drawing room downstairs." We were on the second floor ("It's the first floor in England, Ayako").

"And across the hall is the nursery."

"She's too big for a nursery now."

"Her room then? I thought she and the governess could sleep on the second floor, but Ayako could sleep here and the governess could have the third floor to herself, if that's better."

There was no view of San Francisco Bay from my room, but it did have a fireplace with a carved white mantelpiece, like all the rooms, even the ones in the attic, or "second floor." This was something new and I loved the fireplaces from the start; they were so bright and warm. There was nothing like being tucked into bed, watching the flames, and listening to a story.

Ada and Governesses

The tour of the house ended with all of us going down to the dining room on the ground floor and then to the place that interested me most: the basement. Ada and Hana's quarters were here near the huge kitchen. If the rest of the house looked dark, the basement was positively black. I felt as though I were going down steep, dark steps into a cavern. This was a dungeon found in fairy tales—even the Aga was black. And yet this would become the sunniest place in the house for me, a far cry from a witch's hole, and all because of cheerful Ada.

Ada was short and fat, standing only a head higher than I did but with ten times my girth. She huffed and puffed as she waddled up the stairs with platters, trays, brooms. "Oh, me legs" she'd puff, with a laugh. She was always hot, her brown-gray hair always rumpled. ("I wish she'd do something with her appearance when we have guests. Hana looks so crisp in her black uniform and lace cap; you'd never think Ada was wearing the same thing, she looks so untidy. It's embarrassing.")

I was used to Goto shooing me out of the kitchen. ("You're in the way, I'm busy") and the maids in Tokyo turning me away ("Miss Ayako, young ladies shouldn't come into the kitchen"). Ada was always in a good mood. She sang in that black kitchen and she liked to talk—even a child was better than no audience.

Papa was fond of Ada and praised her cooking whenever he truthfully could, which was not often.

"Ada, today's lamb is excellent."

She'd beam, cap askew. "I can do English cooking, French cooking, and Japanese cooking. Mr. Yasuda, I worked for 'im before I came here, said me *tempura* was the best he ever ate."

I loved to sneak down to the kitchen to watch Ada and listen to her stories. She always welcomed me, no matter how busy she was, and treated me as an equal. She was at her best in the afternoons, sitting in a corner of the darkness, gaily sipping tea from a large mug or even more gaily drinking ale. ("Shu, I think Ada *drinks* in the afternoon. I could smell it when she served dinner." "Probably does—they all do. But you won't find a harder-working and more loyal person than Ada, even if her cooking is more home style than French, so I'd ignore the pint now and then." "Maybe you're so broad-minded because you like a tipple yourself? But you're right, it doesn't interfere with her duties, and she's a good soul.")

"Ada, I'm going to school soon."

"Now, isn't that something—here, have a sardine. If I were a big girl like you, I'd have gone to school long ago."

"I don't like school, and this sardine smells fishy."

"Fishy! Hand it back!" Ada popped the mutilated sardine into her own mouth and licked her fingers "Mmm...love sardines. Loved school, too. You know, once me and me friends, we went on a school trip and after 'lights out' we talked and talked," she said, then tee-hee-heed and perched on the table. "We were terribly hungry, and one of the girls had brought a can of sardines, so we crawled into her bed, squeezed under her blanket, and using a torchlight—"

"How could you all fit under one blanket?"

"Now you're a sly one." Ada wagged her finger. "I was a wee thing then, skinnier than you are, but we were *packed* under that blanket as tightly as (tee-hee-hee) these sardines. Maybe the corners weren't tucked in, but we crouched there, and no sardines ever tasted as good. We gobbled them in a minute."

A new glamour surrounded the sardines. I picked one out of Ada's can and popped it into my mouth. Tasty and exciting. The sardines *were* tightly packed. I imagined two rows of Adas tightly packed together and liked the picture. I ate another sardine.

I did not go to school for the first year because my parents wished to avoid a repeat of my San Francisco fiasco. They wanted me to learn English and English customs beforehand so that I would blend in well at school. For this I had a series of governesses.

"Much easier than the way I learned the English way of life." Mama sounded amused.

Papa laughed. "The first time we came here, your mother stayed with two English sisters, retired schoolteachers. She'd never been abroad, and this was her father's brainstorm after talking with some foreign office friend of his. He was a busybody, but he meant well. Your mother lost ten pounds during a crash course of polite English, genteel manners, rice pudding...and I had to become a bachelor again!"

"I had my revenge, though, and felt quite superior to your father when we traveled to Ireland afterwards and went sightseeing on horseback!"

"Ouch, I still feel sore just thinking about that. There was this beautiful spot that we could only reach on horseback, and your mother, an accomplished rider, galloped away with our guide. My mount wanted to keep up, so I had to wrap my arms around his neck and hang on for dear life!"

"Staying at home and learning English and English ways from a governess is much easier, Ayako."

The first three governesses left no impression on me, except that Mama was very upset each time one left.

"Miss Robins said Ayako was rude, that she talked back. She didn't want such a charge and she was quite rude herself."

"Ada said Miss Gibbons was unclean, that she bathed only once during the ten days she was here and left grimy rings around the bathtub."

"Miss Walker said the living arrangements were too cramped, said it had been a mistake to work for a Japanese family."

The fourth governess I immediately liked. Miss Warner was young and pretty, with shoulder-length flaming hair and pretty dresses instead of sensible skirts and blouses. She was also easy-going and a skillful weaver of romantic tales. I spent many happy bedtimes staring into the fire and listening to Miss Warner read from her own book.

"Lucinda sat on the bench in the rose garden. She was engaged to Mortimer, because her parents had always wanted them to marry, but she could not love him. What should she do? A sigh escaped her soft lips as she watched the water dancing in the fountain. Suddenly, she heard footsteps! She was not alone! As she swiftly turned around, she saw a young stranger. He was tall, with golden hair and a face like a prince…"

Miss Warner looked so pretty as she sat on the floor in front of the fire that I was sure that Lucinda was Miss Warner. Story time was sometimes spoiled by our new Scottie, Prince, secretly tucked into bed with me against his will. He'd often fart, and once he even peed on the sheets.

A month after she came, Miss Warner packed and left without saying good-bye.

"Mama, why did Miss Warner leave? I liked her."

"I know. That's why I kept her on though you weren't learning much. I rarely saw her teaching you English. No discipline, either, even letting that filthy Prince into your bed although I expressly forbade her to do so. Who knows what diseases you might have caught."

"That's because I begged her to."

"And well, there was another reason."

"What?"

"I don't want to talk about such things in front of a little girl."

"What? Tell me. I'm big now."

"Well, since you must have a reason…she took things."

"That's not true!"

"I didn't believe it either, though Ada was telling me she did. Then I caught her going through my purse. Let's forget about such things, shall we? She's gone, and she seems to have told you many good stories."

Mama took some time before deciding on the next governess.

"I was talking to Lady Leigh-Roberts about our problem, Shu. I've interviewed several governesses and they all have good references, but I can't seem to decide. I don't have confidence anymore; maybe I just don't know how to treat English governesses, because I don't think Ayako could be that bad."

I felt guilty because I was glad to have no governess.

"Lady Leigh-Roberts said she knew just the right person. She said her daughter didn't need a governess anymore and that she might be interested in coming here."

"But, Hide, I don't think a governess for the Leigh-Roberts would come to us."

"That's what I said, too, but she sounded pretty confident."

"Well, you know how Sir Henry is always so cordial. Most Englishmen now are put off with the war in China—they are pro-Chinese, so it's hard for a Japanese diplomat to do his duty with that wall of cold resistance—but Sir Henry has good memories of his travels in Japan. I don't want to create trouble for him, though, make him unpopular because of his friendship with me…"

"You said he spent a year in Japan after he finished Oxford?"

"Yes, before he started working at the bank."

Lady Leigh-Roberts must have been persuasive, because Miss Hamilton became my next and last governess.

Mama was apologetic. "I'm afraid this is very different from the Leigh-Roberts's, and Ayako may be difficult at times."

"I don't expect any of that to be a problem, ma'am. It is our duty to deal with difficult children."

"I'm glad you feel that way."

Miss Hamilton and I sized each other up. She saw a sallow, six-year-old Oriental child with sullen mouth and an insecure look. I saw a woman with calm brown eyes who dressed sensibly, like my first three governesses, and carried herself with an air of complete confidence. It would be hard to get rid of her.

Miss Hamilton took the smaller attic room. No thank you, she needed no sitting room as she would be returning to her home on weekends. Lessons started at once, and I had to read and write every day. There weren't too many stories, but there was a lot about what nice girls did not say or do.

"I've got a dog called Prince. He's got black hair and black eyes."

"Yes, Prince has black hair and black eyes, but 'got' is American and not good English. Use 'have' and 'has.' Repeat: 'I have a dog called Prince. He has black hair and black eyes.'"

"All right."

"'Yes, Miss Hamilton,' please. That is what will be expected at school."

"Yes, Miss Hamilton. 'I have a dog called Prince.' It's hot here, I'm sweating. Can I open the window?"

"Yes you may. I was thinking of doing it myself, because it is rather warm, but ladies do not sweat," Miss Hamilton said as she wrinkled her nose in disgust, "they perspire. Even then, you need not *say* it. Just say it's warm, not hot, and that you'd like to open the window."

"You're so fussy. I hate you!"

"Young ladies never hate, they *dislike*."

"Hate, hate, hate!"

"We'll have no more of this nonsense. I am here to teach you English and English manners. Your mother wants you to be a well-behaved young lady." There was something in Miss Hamilton's dry voice and disapproving eye that checked me more than her anger could have. She was not cold or unkind; she was disappointed and pitied me. I could not bear to be pitied.

Miss Hamilton was a great believer in walks, where she often told stories, though never about her own life or Lucinda and the tall, blonde stranger. I heard about Peter Rabbit, Winnie-the-Pooh and Alice's Adventures in Wonderland, stories that we'd read later in our warm house. The wind and the rain stung my face.

"We must put some color in those cheeks of yours." Unless there was a storm, we walked every afternoon. "A little bit of rain never hurt anyone. The English girl's peaches-and-cream complexion comes from fresh air and exercise."

I quite liked to walk in Regent's Park and Hyde Park in fair weather, but we tramped the streets more often than not.

"You must get your bearings for when you go to school."

Some streets were crowded and noisy. Mostly it was raining—I cannot remember ever being hot (warm?) and sweating (perspiring). I guess the three months she tried to make me into a nice English girl was wintertime.

We walked past stores, crossed intersections.

"Remember never to speak to anyone to whom you have not been introduced. A stranger might be a bad man, ready to whisk you away."

"Hello, dearies. Wet 'haint it for a mite of fresh air?" The workman doffed his cap and smiled, revealing two missing teeth.

We walked by, heads held high.

We returned with rosy cheeks and sparkling eyes for tea and scones in my playroom. Miss Hamilton poured tea.

"Would you like milk or lemon?"

"Milk, please."

"Sugar?"

"Five, please. No, six, please."

"I do think three would be more than enough, Ayako."

We sipped our tea, little finger crooked, and I tried not to gobble my scones.

"Now, let's see you curtsey to one of your mother's friends in your pretty frock."

I brushed aside my crumbs and curtsied deeply.

"Ve-ery good. Not like a chambermaid's bob nor the way your mother will be curtseying to the Queen."

Miss Hamilton left, but not because of any unpleasantness.

"I'll be saying goodbye next week, Ayako, and I will miss you."

I looked up with surprise. "Why are you leaving?"

"You have made remarkable progress, though I must admit, you were quite a challenge! Now you behave as well as any well-brought-up English girl. That is, when you choose to. Your English is quite good, too. You'll be going to Frances Holland School at Clarence Gate and you'll make many friends there and you won't need me any longer." Miss Hamilton looked surprisingly mild. "I have other things to do also, Ayako, but I'll be thinking of you. So remember, sit up straight like the Queen Mother Mary, as if you were wearing tight corsets, and never speak to strangers."

The Coronation

Mama was also practicing her curtseying, performing deep curtseys before the mirror.

"Are you going to be presented to the Queen?"

Mama laughed. "How did you know? All diplomats' wives are presented soon after they arrive, but in my case, it's been postponed till after the coronation. But I have to prepare; it's been so long since I was presented the first time we were in England."

For some time there had been talk around our house of King Edward and "that Simpson woman," and more recently, a buzz about his abdication and the coronation of King George VI.

"They were talking about the abdication at the club when I walked in," Papa had said one evening to Mama. "I could tell by the way they all clammed up and looked glum. Sir Walter and I talked about the weather and golf, and as I was leaving, I told him how deeply I sympathized with him for the loss of such a popular king. He took my hand and said, 'Thank you for understanding. This is a dark time for us.' They had been so proud of their King Edward, and now to have him abdicate for an American divorcee!"

I looked at newspaper pictures of the Simpson woman. She was a vivid contrast of black and white: dark hair, white face, dark eyes and lips, white shoulders, dark dress, and a full smile. She was quite glamorous, and the Royals looked washed out in comparison.

"I think she's very beautiful."

"Beautiful?!" Mama was indignant. "The Duchess of Kent has grace and beauty, but Mrs. Simpson..."

"Still, she must be very seductive," said Papa, "for the king to have given up his throne for her."

Then the days became more and more festive, with streets garlanded for the coronation. Papa and Mama were quite excited by the prospect of seeing this historic event, and there was much hustle and bustle in the house. Ada was given the day off "to catch a glimpse o' me new King and Queen," and only Hana and I remained at home.

"How was it, how was it?" I wanted to know the details the next day, and poured over the pictures in the special section of the papers.

"It was magnificent," Papa said, smiling. "Nobody can surpass the British in ceremonies and pageants, and it was a welcome change to rejoice."

"King George looked much more reserved than King Edward, but Queen Elizabeth smiled all the time, so gracious. And didn't you think the two princesses were sweet, Shu, dressed identically in their crowns and ermine-trimmed capes? They say Margaret Rose wanted the same dress as her sister and that King George could deny his youngest nothing."

I looked at the pictures of the two princesses waving from the balcony with the King and Queen. Princess Elizabeth was frowning slightly, but they were very pretty, especially Margaret Rose (what a nice name). Princess Elizabeth was exactly the same age as Masa and Margaret Rose was my age.

"I stood on me toes and caught a glimpse of the carriages. Cinderella coaches, they were," Ada told me in the kitchen. "Then we danced in the street and went on to the White Hart! Such a celebration! Laughing and singing and everyone treated a pint. I could hardly roll out of me bed this morning!" She waltzed and handed me tabloids full of pictures of carriages, the Royal Family, cheering crowds, flags, and other foreign kings, queens, princes, and princesses. "From Japan, too," said Ada.

Some time afterwards, Mama was presented at court. Mama looked like a queen herself as she left the house, wearing a long white and silver lace dress embroidered with beads and pearls, with a matching train, a pearl tiara, long white gloves and an ostrich fan.

Again, the next morning, I wanted to hear all about it. "Show me how you curtseyed."

Mama curtseyed to the ground.

"You must have been the prettiest person with the prettiest dress."

"Don't be silly, Ayako. Other diplomats' wives were much more beautiful, with magnificent jewelry, but I must say, the dress was all right."

Papa came in. "No wonder, with all the fittings. At the first fitting the train was thrown out, beads and all, as being too short. No altering or scrimping there."

"Well, you know the Japanese physique. Western women do have more presence than Oriental women."

"Fishing for compliments, that's what you are. You're very attractive and you know it."

Mama was slender and tall for a Japanese woman, with long legs. I wished I had Mama's deep-set eyes and slender nose.

"When you grow up you'll be beautiful, like your mother," Miss Hamilton and Miss Warner had said. I could not see how an ugly duckling like myself could be so transformed into a swan.

"The Queen was smiling and very gracious when Ambassador Yoshida's wife presented me, but I was so nervous that I don't remember what we talked about."

My life revolved around the Bayswater house and garden, with Papa, Mama, and Ada. Hana remained in the background and Prince had died of distemper. I was to enter Frances Holland School next term, but I was quite happy just to be at home, as I had become used to the dark house and the damp garden, with its so many nooks and surprises

When Papa was at home, I'd coax him to act out some fairy tales with me. Ada was enlisted and Mama and Hana were reluctant extras. "Cinderella" and "Sleeping Beauty" were my favorites. I dressed up in Mama's clothes to be Cinderella, Papa was the Prince, and Ada would be scolded for laughing as she played the wicked stepmother.

Once I made up my own play where the Prince is saved by the Princess from being poisoned by her stepmother. For this I created a dessert in Ada's kitchen.

"An apple jelly'd be more to your father's taste."

"No, I want to make a butter jelly." I liked the creamy feel and the yellow color and did not taste it—it was supposed to be poisoned anyway.

The Prince sat at the dining table. The stepmother served him the poisoned dessert. It was golden and had been perfectly turned out from a small jelly mould.

"I made this with my own lily-white hands," the stepmother giggled.

"How good it looks," said the Prince, putting a spoonful into his mouth.

"No, no!" screamed the Princess, rushing in. "It is poisoned!"

The Prince gagged, spit out the dessert onto his plate, and made a face.

"You were perfect, Papa!"

"What did you put in this, Ada?!" Papa wiped his tongue and drank some water.

"*I* made it, not Ada. It's butter jelly; isn't it lovely?"

"Ugh."

"Really, Ada," said Mama, "you could have taught her something better."

"She's a stubborn lass, ma'am."

Outside, behind the gooseberry, blackberry, and elderberry bushes, there was a corner left wild, with black-eyed susans and once a discarded boot among the weeds.

On wet days I was told to play in the concrete laundry yard, where Ada could see my feet from the kitchen window. (Mama was mindful of Miss Hamilton's belief that fresh air built character as well as a peaches-and-cream skin). Unlike the garden, it was boring here. I played with my ball and skipping rope, but there were no trees, bushes, or flowers. Instead, there were spiders near the basement window, large black ones that I feared. I missed my walks with Miss Hamilton and would not mind going to school after all.

Frances Holland School

I was enrolled at Frances Holland School on the recommendation of Lady Leigh-Roberts.

"It's supposed to be a very good girls' school," said Mama.

Papa snorted, "I hope it won't be so good that Ayako won't fit in and you'll do something as rash as you did with Masa's school in Japan."

"With Masa, I thought he fit in quite well; it was the teachers who were narrow-minded. Can you imagine Mr. Ueda lecturing me that it was the height of rudeness to be spilling rice grains in front of Prince Kaya, that if Masa didn't know how to handle his chopsticks because he had lived abroad, I should pack a spoon in his lunchbox. The Peeress's School in my days wasn't so rigid. You'd think Masa had committed *lèse majesté* instead of a trifle. I'm sure the Prince himself didn't care."

"If it was a trifle, why did you pull him out of the Peers School and put him into Seikei? Maybe Mr. Ueda just wanted you to put a spoon in until you taught Masa to use chopsticks better?"

"It wasn't just because of the chopsticks. I had been thinking that with our international background, we should put him in a school where he could be freer, not be told, 'You must forget all your English and become a true Japanese son of Imperial Japan.' I like the Seikei boys and graduates, not too conservative, but not 'smelling of butter' either, very natural and easy going."

"I was only joking. You're right, you took a wise if rather drastic step. However, remember the temper of the times, Hide, and don't be disappointed if Masa's hearing a lot about being a 'real Japanese' at Seikei too."

"I wish we could have him here with us."

Papa sighed. "You know as well as I do that a boy has to have a Japanese education or he'll never be accepted into Japanese society. He wouldn't be accepted abroad either—he'd be 'neither fish nor fowl' and unhappy. Thirty years from now, things may be different, but look at Count Shirai's son or Mr. Furukawa's son: they drink, gamble, play around—charming lost playboys with no roots. If Masa could come during the holidays, that would be ideal, but vacation time would be over on board ship; just getting here takes so much time."

"How about Ayako, then?"

"She's a girl and she'll marry, and besides, neither you nor I could bear to be away from both children. Let's hope she won't have to find a job and fight in the big, hard world."

Papa and Mama suddenly remembered I was there and listening.

Mama smiled. "You'll like your school. Your English is good and you'll make lots of friends."

I took the bus to Frances Holland School with Ada ("Just hold on till I get me hat") or with Hana when Ada was busy; Hana didn't like to speak English.

Classes were quiet, long, and dull.

"She has a beautiful English accent, but her vocabulary is still rather limited. She should read more."

I liked the activities outside the classroom best.

Lunch was a welcome break despite the formal setting in the refectory: a large, dark room with long tables and benches (to ensure we would not lean back). The teachers sat at the ends of each table, so there was always a small scramble to sit in the middle next to a good friend. I almost elbowed others aside to sit next to Zara, who told wonderful stories, was pretty and popular, and had a smile like sunshine. Zara's mother was American and very glamorous, like 'that Simpson woman,' but very nice too, with a different accent. Zara didn't have any accent; she'd never been to America. It was Katya who complicated things by wanting to sit next to me.

"Mama, Katya is so sticky and uninteresting."

"Now, Ayako, Katya and her parents left Czechoslovakia only a year ago and are having a hard time adjusting here, so be nice to her."

"But her English is better than mine."

"She had an English governess, but they haven't made many friends yet."

"Well *I* don't want to be a friend with sticky Katya."

"Don't you remember your kindergarten days in San Francisco, when you were so unhappy without good friends? Be nice to her."

That silenced me. I tried to keep out of Katya's way but tolerated her when we were thrown together.

Lunch itself consisted of soup, boiled meat, and vegetables with a generous helping of potatoes, bread, and finally dessert. I always looked forward to dessert.

"Goody, goody, today's Monday, so it's rice pudding, though Mama thinks rice with milk is disgusting."

Zara chanted, "Mondays rice pudding, Tuesdays stewed apricots and prunes, Wednesdays bread pudding, Thursdays rhubarb, and Fridays trifle. I like Fridays best; rice pudding is revolting."

"I hate, I mean, I dislike Thursdays. Rhubarb is so *sour*. Trifle is all right."

Miss Temple, faraway at the end of the table, heard everything she wanted to hear above the chatter of voices. "Ayako, rhubarb cleans your blood and is good for you. Zara, it is vulgar for young ladies to be talking about food so much."

I also looked forward to our walks in Regent's Park. The locker room was a flurry of anticipation before we marched, in pairs. Change your shoes, put on your blazer, gloves, and hat in a hurry in order to line up and choose your partner: first ready, first to choose. If a shoe was forgotten under a bench, you had to go back to put it away and you lost your place. There would always be whispers:

"Will you be my partner today?"

"I already promised Marian."

"Don't choose me today. I want to walk with Jane."

"But I want you to walk with *me*."

"I'll never forgive you if you call my name, because I'm going with Jane."

Miss Temple frowned impatiently. "Hurry up, girls, or we won't have time to go to the park!"

I tried to go with Zara, but most of the time some other girl called out "Zara!" or "Ayako!" before we got together. It was all right to go with others, too, as long as it wasn't Katya, because there were lots of nice girls. Besides, walking itself was such fun (unlike Miss Hamilton, Miss Temple did not take us in the rain). It was a chance to get out of school and see all sorts of different people and flowers and trees.

Some girls remained unchosen till the end, one fat girl especially, and I always felt guilty, but I didn't want to walk with Louise, either. At times, Miss Temple beckoned a girl before we entered the locker room, saying, "Zara, choose Louise" or "Ayako, walk with Louise," and we obeyed glumly. Louise walked with downcast eyes and didn't talk much. There was another girl, Carol, whom nobody chose because of her rough manners and twangy accent, and this made her cross and even rougher. One afternoon, Carol was two girls behind me. I recognized her nasal voice.

"Why do you talk like that?" Carol's partner, Margaret, asked.

"Like what?"

"Like this." Margaret pinched her own nose and said, "I'm Canadian. I like Canada better than England."

The girls behind me tittered.

"I *am* Canadian, and Canada is much better than stupid England."

"Oooh! You talk funny."

"*You* talk funny, and how about Ayako. She's Japanese." Carol stuck her tongue out at me.

"But she doesn't talk funny like you do," said Margaret. "She speaks *English*."

I remained silent. I wanted to hoot with my friends, but something held me back. Carol punched Margaret.

"Ouch!" There was a scuffle.

Miss Temple stopped the line. "What's going on back there? Carol, come up here in front with me. Margaret, go to the back of the line and walk by yourself."

Another afternoon, Miss Temple said we could play "drop the handkerchief" in Regent's Park, because we had made good time. Hardly had we begun when I spotted Papa walking with another Japanese man. They were deep in talk, both in business suits.

"It's Papa! Miss Temple, that's my Papa!" I ran up to Papa, who looked up in surprise, came over to Miss Temple, and introduced himself while his friend sat down on a far bench. I noticed Miss Temple was all smiles.

"Well, I don't want to keep you girls from your game." Papa waved his hand at the circle of uniforms and started to walk away.

The game continued, then everyone started looking at me, giggling. I looked back to find that Papa had dropped his handkerchief behind me and was laughing, waiting for me to pick it up and run. Five minutes of shrieks and dashes followed, with Papa running full speed with us in his dark suit, dropping his handkerchief behind Miss Temple, Zara, Katya, Louise, then he ran away to his friend, waving.

"Your father's so nice!"

"I wish my daddy would play with me like that."

"Aren't you lucky!"

I fairly burst with pride.

At school you could take piano lessons and dancing lessons.

"So, you will become graceful young ladies." Miss Temple approved.

I took both, but by now found piano boring, with its Czerny and finger exercises. I was said to play well, however, and was to appear in the school concert, what I would remember afterwards as the "blue dress recital."

"There are only two more weeks to the concert. Practice every day at home, girls, and remember to wear a white dress on the big day."

I went home and looked at my white dress. It was piqué, with tucks. Quite chic, said Mama. My eyes went to the dress I had begged Mama to buy at Harrods: it was of the lightest blue organdy, with ruffles on the wide skirt and ruffles on the puffed sleeves. It had a rustling taffeta petticoat. That would be the dress I'd wear! Wasn't the blue very pale?

"Are you sure it's all right?" Mama sounded doubtful, but I had made up my mind.

Ten girls sat in the wings waiting to play our pieces. Miss Lewis, our piano teacher, frowned. "I said white, Ayako." However, she was too busy to give me a real scolding. "Oh well, it's too late to do anything now."

"What a pretty dress, Ayako."

"You're wearing blue. Don't you have a white dress?"

I hadn't thought my blue organdy dress would cause such a fuss and began to wish I had chosen the white piqué.

When I went on stage, I was surprised at the number of people in the school auditorium; but oh well, I thought, there wasn't much difference between playing for Miss Lewis or for a sea of faces. I played with aplomb and curtseyed to loud applause.

"Who's the Chinese girl?"

"The girl in blue is very good."

After the performance, grownups came up to me as I joined Papa and Mama.

"You were very good, so natural."

"You should be a pianist when you grow up."

"And such a pretty dress."

Miss Lewis was all smiles and did not scold me. The other little pianists were not so forgiving.

"You wore blue so as to get all the attention!"

"You wanted to be different!

So much fuss over a blue organdy dress.

The dance performance would be something very special, we had been told over and over again. We were one of the schools to appear for charity in a real theatre, and Princess Margaret Rose would grace us with her presence. In our specially-made tunics, we Grecian maidens sat stiffly backstage.

"Posture young ladies, posture! How many of you sit up straight like the Queen Mother Mary when you are at home?"

Queen Mary again! I started to raise my hand but pretended to scratch my nose when no other hands were raised and I heard the guilty giggling to my left and right.

"No, I didn't think any of you did. Remember, Grecian maidens all have good posture." Miss Warren did not sound surprised at all as the girls slouched, showing how they sat at home. I too giggled and slouched so as not to be different. If others hadn't sat up straight like Queen Mary, why had I? How stupid I had been.

There were many groups going onstage and our piece was over in minutes, receiving loud applause, nobody caring whether we slouched or not.

"She's sitting over there." I squinted to look into the box indicated but saw only darkness.

Afterwards, Princess Margaret Rose came backstage and we all curtseyed.

"A great honor," whispered Miss Warren. "Be on your best behavior, girls."

Princess Margaret Rose wanted to have everything the same as her sister, Mama had said. We were all presented with a gold medal that said "for service," and I placed mine in my trinket box as my greatest treasure.

Mama and Papa

Mama and Papa seemed to have even more friends than I did, English and Japanese. Dinner parties were frequent and at breakfast there was always talk of the previous evening.

"I was never so embarrassed in my life. If there had been a hole I would have slunk into it," Mama said one morning.

"Don't worry, I'm the one who looked a fool. It's the host's business to know his wines." Papa was laughing. "Did you see Sir John flinch when he swallowed that brandy? Being a gentleman, 'Most unusual' was his only comment, an understatement if there ever was one. I was puzzled until I took a sip of it myself!"

"How could Ada have mixed up our Courvoisier with cooking brandy!"

"Oh well, we all had a good laugh, and Sir John's tastebuds were soothed with the right brandy—and quite a bit of it, too."

Papa and Mama were often invited by their English friends, many of them from my parents' previous days in London.

"Ayako, we were invited to the preview of *Gone with the Wind* last night," Mama said with stars in her eyes. "It was the most gorgeous film I ever saw." This was a year after the brandy incident.

"Yes," agreed Papa, "the color, the setting, the acting were all beautiful. A new era in cinema has begun. It's not all romance either; the horrors of war is a timely theme."

"Clark Gable was so dashing and Vivien Leigh so lovely. Champagne was served during intermission and everyone toasted the two stars. It was much longer than other films and we had to have an intermission, a chance to celebrate."

"I never saw anything after *Little Miss Marker* and *Captain Blood*. Can't I go to the cinema, too? Not just to pantos?"

"When that *Snow White* comes, you'll be going with your friends."

"Will it come soon?"

"Let's hope so."

Prince and Princess Chichibu visited England in 1937. The Prince was an avid sports lover and the Princess had lived in London as a child and spoke perfect English. They were well-loved members of the Imperial Family and their goodwill visit was hoped to bring much-needed friendship.

Papa and Mama were kept very busy and I saw little of them during this period. These Imperial visitors who took up so much of my parents' time—what were they like? I wondered.

I managed to catch a glimpse of the Imperial guests at the Hurlingham Club when I took part in a tug-of-war with the other Japanese children. "Be on your best behavior!" You always had to be on your best behavior in front of princes and princesses, and that was very difficult in a tug-of-war. Their Imperial Highnesses came down from the stands afterwards and talked to us.

"Oh, so this is the Tomiis' daughter. How like your mother you look," the Princess said, and smiled. I curtseyed, remembering too late that I was to bow. Flustered, I did not glance up, and it was only later that I took a long look at them in the photograph on our piano.

Framed in silver, the sports-loving Prince was in uniform and looked studious and frail. The Princess, with a semi-smile, reminded me of the Duchess of Kent. They both seemed calm and gracious.

Shadows of War

Of course, all was not sunshine and laughter, for it was now 1938. Heather Baines and Fiona Smith never played with me, but they came up to me one day, noses held high.

"My father says I'm not to play with you because you're Japanese."

"The Japanese are *bad*. They're killing the Chinese. Someday we're going to kill all of you, bam-bam-bam."

"Nip, Nip with slanty eyes."

That evening, I asked, "Papa, why are the Japanese killing the Chinese?"

"Where did you hear that?"

"Heather and Fiona say the Japanese are bad and they're not to play with me."

"Ah, the parents talk about it and the children repeat it at school. You wouldn't understand yet, Ayako."

"Yes, I would."

"How should I put it. Japan is becoming a modern country, like England and America, and it needs more resources, more land. But there is no space that does not already belong to someone else, so there's fighting. And when there's fighting, lots of very bad things happen—people lose their homes, people are killed."

"Then why is Japan bad and not China."

"The Japanese are in China and not the Chinese in Japan, but that's a long story. Besides, England and China are friends."

Mama and Papa had been excited for weeks and I soon learned why.

"We're moving to Canada, Ayako. What do you think of that?" said Papa.

I thought of Carol with her funny accent. We'd all be speaking like that. "Where is Canada?"

"Canada is across the sea, next to America. We're going to Ottawa, where your mother and I lived with Masa in 1928 and 1929, so we have many friends there from those days. Come to think of it, in 1928 we sailed from England to Canada, too. What a coincidence."

"Friends! I'd have to leave Zara and Margaret and Sarah and Ann and Nellie and Frances…Ada…even Louise and Katya. "I like England. I like my friends here."

"So do we, and we're sorry to leave England," said Papa, "but if we're going anyway, it may not be a bad time, the way things are in Europe. Besides, it will be good to see our Canadian friends again."

"If only Masa were with us," Mama said with a sigh. "Remember our Saint Bernard, how he used to pull Masa's sled through the streets in Ottawa."

"Yes. Well, Canada is quite a bit nearer to Japan than England. Maybe he could come during the holidays."

"But you said with fighting in China, calling one's son during the holidays would look frivolous."

"Yes it would," Papa said. "People in Japan are leading a Spartan life now, and it wouldn't be right to indulge personal desires too much. Perhaps you could make a short visit to Japan. There's always family business to attend to and it would be a good chance to pray at the Tomii and Nakamura graves…but I suspect that once we reach Canada, you'll be too busy to take that much time off."

I went to Zara Howard's house for tea; it was a small but pretty place, light and airy. In her play box, I found a yellow wig with two long plaits made of wool. I could be a blonde for one afternoon; I would look like my school friends. I had always liked golden hair, though Zara's was a light brown.

Zara howled with laughter. "Oh, you look so *funny*. Ha ha ha HA! Come and show Mummy." She dragged me towards her mother's room. Mrs. Howard was wrapping ornaments in newspapers and putting them in a big crate. She looked at me, shook her real blonde hair, and burst out laughing. Seeing that I was hurt, she said, "You have such beautiful black hair. I wish *I* had your silky black hair! With you features, yellow hair doesn't go very well. Besides, that's only a play wig, and not well made."

I looked at myself in the mirror on the wall and saw that I looked like Minnehaha, who had appeared in one of our stories, except that I had funny yellow plaits.

"You look like Raggedy Ann!" howled Zara, snatching the wig and putting it on her own head. She certainly didn't look like Raggedy Ann, I thought. She looked like a Swedish maiden.

"I wish I had yellow hair like yours, Mrs. Howard. Are you going someplace? Papa says we're going to Canada, and Mama's packing, too

"We'll be close then, because we're going back to America."

"Why are you going to America?"

"I'm American, you know."

"But Zara's English and Mr. Howard's English and you don't talk funny like Carol."

"I've been in England for a long, long time, dear. But the way things are now in Europe, Tom and I want to take Zara to America."

"Papa also said, 'the way things are in Europe'."

"Mummy says there may be war," said Zara.

Mrs. Howard laughed uncomfortably. "Nobody knows, but with Hitler, if there's fighting…"

China and Japan were fighting. England might fight. What did all this mean?

From 1973, I lived in Surrey for seven years. During that time, I tried to find the house on Bayswater Road and Frances Holland School at Clarence Gate. Unlike 2622 Jackson Street, I did not remember the address and could not find the house. Perhaps it had been torn down, or perhaps it had been destroyed in WWII (though being London, chances were it still was standing). My father had died, and my mother couldn't remember the address either, but vivid in her mind was the house and address at St. Petersburgh Place, where my brother was born. I took pictures of the four-story house, now divided into apartments, and my mother looked at them with a nostalgic sigh. Yes, it was the same house, still white with black trimmings. The school was easier to find, but I did not have the courage to go in. I pressed my face to a window and saw a stray shoe. It must have been the locker room—old or new, I do not know.

CANADA

En Route

Certainly the sumptuous SS *Normandie,* on which we sailed from Southampton to New York, put away all thoughts of fighting. With cinema theatre, huge murals, and elevators, it was a floating city.

"I'd really have preferred the SS *Queen Elizabeth*," said Papa, "but the schedule of the *Normandie* was more convenient, and besides, it's her maiden voyage."

"Monsieur *le Ministre* and Mme. are happy with these rooms, *j'espère?*" The steward bowed low as he led us to a creamy, elegant bedroom with an adjoining rattan and chintz sunroom. Next, we were shown a small windowless cabin around a corner. "And this is for the *petite enfante* and her *gouvernante*." No bow.

"Could we not change this room for one facing outside?" Mama asked. "Of course, we will make up the difference."

"I am sorry, Mme. *Baronne*, but all the outside cabins are already taken. This is a very comfortable room for a child and her governess; we thought this would be quite suitable." A shrug.

Next we were shown the dining room, with murals up to the high ceiling, chandeliers, thick carpeting, potted plans, pink tablecloths, and crystal glasses.

"Dinner is served at nine o'clock."

"So late," said Mama. "Past our daughter's bedtime."

"We have a children's dining room down the hall which is open from 12:00 for lunch and 6:00 for dinner. The main dining room is largely for adults."

We looked at the room where Hana and I would have our meals: nothing on the walls, a scattering of pantry-like tables and chairs on a bare floor. Few children seemed to be on board the *Normandie*.

I did not like my cabin and ended up sleeping on the sofa in the sunroom. Hana muttered that she'd feel seasick with no windows, even if she liked having her room to herself.

Mealtimes in our bare dining room were unexpectedly fun. Papa and Mama always took so long when they went for their meals, and I was relieved that Hana and I ate separately, with no need to be on my best behavior since there were no grownups around. Only three children dined at the same hours that we did, and they were about my age: Mariko, Tony, and Elizabeth. We got along well.

"Ice cream for dessert again."

"Ice cream is *cold*. Let's make it cold cream."

"Cold cream, ha, ha."

"Ha, ha. HAH."

"How'll we make it *cold* cream?"

"Put it on the radiator, then the ice cream will become cold cream."

"Wheeeeee." The four of us rushed to melt our dessert on the radiators.

"Disgusting," said Hana.

One night, Mama and Papa, all dressed up and smelling nice, had gone to dinner, and I was being a good girl, tucked in for the evening on the sofa. I was gazing around the sunroom—I really liked the yellow flowers and green leaves on the cushion covers and curtains—when I heard a key in the lock (had Papa or Mama forgotten something? There was a lot of fumbling). I leaned on my elbow and, hidden by the back of the sofa, looked through the glass partition. A man wearing the white jacket of a steward came in, quickly glanced around the room, checked the bathroom, and started opening drawers. What a strange steward. I sank down deeper into the sofa and peered out from the side. He opened and closed all the drawers and went through some papers but took nothing. Mama's pearl necklace was on the dresser and her rings were in the second drawer, but he didn't even glance at them. He opened Papa's briefcase and started looking through the papers inside.

"What are you doing." I tried to sound stern as I got up.

"Oh, pardon, pardon, mademoiselle." He closed the briefcase and backed out of the room fast.

I padded out of the sunroom and poked my head into the corridor, but he was gone. Should I tell Hana? But then I would have to dress, so decided to wait till Papa and Mama returned.

I fell asleep before they came back, so I told them the next morning.

"You must have had a nightmare. There's nothing missing," said Mama.

"I left my attaché case beside the desk, not on that chair." Papa looked thoughtful and opened his briefcase. "Hmmm. Good thing I don't have anything important in here; it was not even worth locking it. He was no ordinary thief."

Papa called the purser and I was asked to repeat what I saw.

"He peered into the bathroom like this, opened the drawers and opened Papa's briefcase like this…" I felt very important.

"What did he look like, mademoiselle?"

"He wore a white jacket like a waiter, had brown hair, and looked ordinary…looked like you."

"Mademoiselle, must be mistaken. Monsieur *le Ministre*, all of our people are carefully chosen and we have no thieves, I am absolutely sure. Perhaps it was a dream?"

"But I saw him. I wasn't asleep, and I talked to him."

"Impossible." He looked at me coldly with disbelief and dislike. After that there were no more break-ins.

In New York my wish to see the cinema was granted when we went to the new Radio City. I was thrilled by the Rockettes and by a film about Irene and Vernon Castle, with Fred Astaire and Ginger Rogers and talked about it for weeks.

Papa wanted to pay his respects to Ambassador Saito, so we went to Washington. At the embassy, I lunched in an alcove with his daughters, Sakiko and Masako, and their governess, little guessing that in 1946 Sakiko would become my classmate in Japan and that in later years, Masako and I would both teach at the Sacred Heart College in Tokyo.

We crossed over to Canada from Niagara Falls after staying overnight on the American side. The rainbow illuminations in the evening were magical. During the day, I donned a yellow mackintosh to go down an elevator to watch the falls from behind the rush of water, then walked over a rickety wooden promontory above the falls.

"Papa, I can't walk, my feet won't move!" As I looked down, the soles of my feet tingled and I became rooted to the spot.

"Give me your hand. It's all right, just don't look down."

I knew now what it was like to be afraid of heights.

The less commercialized Canadian side made up for its lack of glamour with the two mounted policemen who were with the group waiting to welcome us at the border. The scarlet jackets of these genial Mounties were a bright beginning to our stay in Canada.

192 Daly Avenue

One ninety-two Daly Avenue was a corner plot with Victorian manor that looked like a large gingerbread house. Inside, however, it was homey, painted in light colors. The drawing rooms, dining room, family room, and kitchen were on the first floor, and there was a large basement that was used at parties for screening films about Japan. The family bedrooms, my playroom, and the maids' workrooms were upstairs, and the attic had space for servants and several empty rooms. There was a small garden in the front with lawn and with lilac bushes, ideal for hide and seek, which reminded me of *Under the Lilacs* during my Louisa May Alcott phase.

I loved the back garden most, with its warm red brick wall to the left. There were no gooseberry bushes, and at the far end only a picket fence separated it from a sidewalk, but it was drier than the Bayswater garden. Most importantly, the flat lawn became a skating rink in winter.

When he judged that ten inches of snow covered the ground, Jack O'Hara, our chauffeur, hammered together an oblong frame of boards around a large part of the garden, forming our very own skating rink. He lived above the garage to the right of the garden with his wife and two sons.

By the winter of 1939, I was already great friends with Jack and his younger son, Jimmy, who at ten was only a year older than I was.

"May I help, Jack?"

Jack and Jimmy were flattening the snow, making it even inside the frame, adding some here, pinching off some there. "This is too difficult. You've got to have a lot of experience and do it right or you won't have a flat surface. Jimmy and I can do it."

Jimmy was a chip off the old block, with flaming red hair, freckles, and smiling blue eyes. Jack and Jimmy continued to pack the snow carefully to make a level, smooth surface.

"I bet it's going to be clear and cold tonight and it's not going to snow, just the night to hose the rink. You don't want it to snow and make lumps on the ice."

That night through my window, I saw Jack muffled up to his ears in the flood-lit garden, filling the wooden frame halfway to the top with water from the garden hose. By the next morning, a smooth layer of ice had formed. Jack hosed the rink again the second night. The third afternoon, he looked up at the sky.

"I'll skip it tonight; looks like snow."

Sure enough, the rink was blanketed with snow the sunny fourth morning. In the late afternoon, I saw Jack and Jimmy sweeping the snow off the rink.

"Can I help too?"

"Sure, bring a broom and join the brigade."

It was a lot of work, but it was fun to be with Jack and Jimmy.

"You have to sweep off every speck of snow if you want a smooth surface. See, the ice is almost thick enough; you could already skate on it if you wanted to. One more night'll do the trick."

To prove his father's words, Jimmy pirouetted in his galoshes and then stretched his leg behind him in a mock sparrow-pose, all the while holding on to his broom.

"Oh, Jimmy, you're so funny. Do that again."

"Funny? I thought I was like Barbara Ann Scott!" Jimmy pirouetted twice more and threw in a jump for good measure. "Whew, I'm exhausted."

"How about some tea in my igloo?"

Jack had made me an igloo by hollowing out the pile of snow shoveled to the left of the rink, then hosing it.

"Sure." Jimmy crawled in, cocked his little finger, and pretended to sip tea. A scene from a San Francisco park flashed through my mind.

"This is good, but how about some real hot chocolate at my house." We tramped to Jimmy's place, Jack remaining to put the finishing touches on the rink.

"Leave your boots at the bottom of the steps," Mrs. Jack shouted down. Upstairs, smiling, she made large, foaming cups of cocoa, which we drank at the kitchen table.

"It's the best cocoa I ever drank." I blew my nose.

"Thank you. Have some more."

A thin, pale young man in uniform came in. It was Albert, the older son who usually ignored me.

"I never saw you in uniform before. I didn't know you were a soldier."

"I joined up last week." He put on his cap and glared at me. "I'm going to kill a lot of Germans."

"There's too much killing in this world," said Mrs. Jack.

"The Germans are enemies, and this is what I'm going to do to them and their friends." Albert fired an imaginary rifle at me, turned on his heels, and went out.

"Don't pay any attention to him. He just joined and is bursting with enthusiasm."

His words disturbed me, but not for long, for school and school friends were playing bigger and bigger roles in my world.

The Governor General

I went to Elmwood School in Rockliffe Park. Run on the English system, said Mama.

Classes were held in an ordinary schoolish building, but the grounds! There seemed to be endless green—no need to go to a Regents Park for a walk. There was a hockey field that became a skating rink in winter and bushes and trees and slopes where we could play all the hide and seek we wanted. Any walks were for nature study, to learn about trees, nuts, birds, and squirrels.

"You have a funny accent," my classmates said at the beginning. *They* were the ones with funny accents, like Carol's.

"You talk like Lord Tweedsmuir!" one girl laughed.

That evening I asked Papa, "Who's Lord Tweedsmuir?"

"He's the governor general, King George's highest representative in Canada. He's also known as John Buchan, author of mystery books like *The Thirty-Nine Steps*. Very gifted. Why?"

"The girls say I speak like him."

"Ha, ha, ha, you should take it as a compliment. He speaks the King's English."

I met Lord Tweedsmuir twice. The first time was on the skating rink of Government House. Diplomats' families were allowed to use the huge outdoor rink, five times the size of the one at the Minto Club, where Barbara Ann Scott practiced.

A tall gentleman who had been tracing leisurely eights stopped to talk to me.

"Do you enjoy skating?"

"I love it, especially here, because the rink is so big."

"Yes, it is a good-sized rink, I must say. What is your name, young lady?"

"Ayako Tomii. And what is yours?"

"Tweedsmuir is my name."

"The Governor General!" I curtseyed. "Thank you very much for letting me skate here."

"Not at all. A pleasure. So you know who I am. I know your father quite well."

"The girls at school say I talk like you."

"Ha, ha. Wha…What an honour…for me."

"Why do you wear white skates?" I pointed at Lord Tweedsmuir's rather long, immaculate skating shoes. "Only girls wear white boots."

"So they do. I see yours are white. Do I look 'sissy'?"

"Well, men wear black skates. Maybe you should get black ones so as not to look sissy."

"Maybe you're right. It wouldn't do for the governor general to look 'sissy,' would it?"

"No, it wouldn't."

Lord Tweedsmuir repeated the story to Papa and Mama at a dinner.

"Most rude of you, Ayako. You embarrassed me."

Papa laughed. "Lord Tweedsmuir was quite amused and said you curtseyed and thanked him before mentioning his white skating shoes."

"Still, Shu, he's the governor general."

So, when I went to the Christmas party for diplomats' children at Government House (I was seeing *Snow White* for the fifth time, but what could I do), I stayed at the very back, well out of sight.

"Ah, my little friend of the skating rink!" Lord Tweedsmuir appeared from the back. "You see, I have on black shoes today." He was wearing a dark suit and, yes, black shoes. "I don't see you very often there these days, but then I don't go much myself, so maybe we've missed each other?"

I curtseyed and mumbled, "Awfully busy at school these days. This is a lovely party."

"Glad you're enjoying yourself. Wonderful film. I was terrified by the Queen."

I smiled politely and stopped myself from saying that I had already seen it four times at birthday parties.

Friends

School was for studying, I knew, but did as little of it as possible.

"*Ann of Green Gables* is so well written and interesting, girls." I much preferred *Little Women*. Jo and Beth were so much more interesting than that goody-goody Ann. Other favorites were *Lassie Come Home* and *The Secret Garden*.

I quite liked history, though. Once I was so held by a story in a history book that I missed the bell for a test and had to start when everyone was halfway through.

There were Frannie, Jean, Estelle, Janet, Dot, and Laura. My best friend, Frannie, had freckles and a big smile and was our champion at running, climbing trees, field hockey, ice-skating, and skiing. Jean was a tamer version of Frannie. Estelle reminded me of Zara with her prettiness and charm. Janet, Mama's friend's daughter, was not boring like most of mother's friends' daughters. Janet was two years older than I was, but never acted superior and was even better than Frannie at field hockey, ice-skating, and skiing. Dot was a daughter of another friend of Mama. Dot was big and fat and clumsy. She was shy but very kind. She reminded me a bit of Louise, so now I was kind instead of impatient. Laura Browning was famous for her parties—her sleigh parties, skating parties, magic show parties—all at her oak-paneled house with gardens even bigger than the school grounds. She was clever and pretty with dark brown eyes and ringlets that she wrapped in navel orange tissues every night

"Since Michael Browning lost his wife, there's nothing he won't do for his daughter," Papa had said.

In the concrete yard outside the changing room, Frannie and I played jacks as we waited to be fetched. Janet and Jean walked home, as they lived nearby. Laura lived close too, but her father would not let her go home without a grownup.

Sometimes we played bolo. *Boing, boing, boing.* The rubber string pulled the ball back against the paddle again and again. There were variations as well, for example, using both sides. *Boing, put, boing, put...*

"In large bolo contests, people hit the ball five hundred, six hundred times," said Frannie, chewing gum. I never chewed gum, because Papa so hated to see me chomping.

There seemed to be birthday parties every other week. Laura Browning's was in the first week of February. There was a big sleigh, with sleigh bells, pulled by two horses. Ten of us clambered in, covering ourselves with fur rugs as we flew over the snow, laughing, singing, with sleigh bells ringing. Glowing, we came in to hot chocolate and a birthday feast.

"Blow out the candles, Laura!"

"Make a wish!"

"What're you going to wish, Laura?"

"D'you know there's a secret passageway behind this panel?"

"I don't believe you. Laura, is Estelle telling the truth?"

"She showed me the last time I was here."

"Maybe there's a corpse in there!"

Not to be "on one's best behavior" during the feast was a treat, especially after school lunches. The day before was Friday, French table day. Our class sat at Mme. Hervé's table, and because only French could be spoken, we were especially quiet on Fridays. I never said anything unless spoken to. Mme. Hervé had white hair and twittered like a bird. I was enjoying my favorite school dessert: pink junket with multicolored sprinklings and a smell of face powder. Thursday it had been tapioca.

"*Ayako, n'avez vous rien à me dire aujourd'hui?*"

I said the first thing that came into my head.

"*Quel âge avez vous, Mme.?*"

"*Vous ne devriez jamais demander l' âge d'une dame. Cela ne se fait pas. Vous ne devriez parler que de choses d'intérêt général.*"

"But isn't it of general interest?" Giggles.

"*Silence! Continuez en français et ne discutez pas.*"

Birthdays and Christmases had always been happy times, but Halloween was a new experience.

"I want to dress up as a fairy, Mama, with silver hair and a silver wand." I wore a ballet costume, white satin with a tutu, wore silver slippers, and held a wand that Mama had made, with a silver star on the end. Best of all, Mama had made me a white cotton-wool wig like those on her French dolls. I stood inside the front door beside the barrel of apples and the tray of lollipops.

Ping, pong, rang the bell. "Trick or treat!" shouted the witches, goblins, ghosts, cowboys, and circus girls. "How pretty! What a beautiful fairy costume!"

Ping, pong. "Trick or treat!"

"My, you look nice!"

"Come and show it to everyone, come with us!"

"But who'll give out the treats then?"

Papa came out from the drawing room. "Hello, children. Thank you for inviting Ayako—what a brilliant idea. I'll hand out the lollipops and apples. Run along and have a good time."

"Is it safe?" asked Mama.

"Oh, just down the street with these children. It'll be fun to go trick or treating."

"All right, but put on your Red Riding Hood cape, Ayako, otherwise you'll catch cold."

So the fairy put on her red velvet cape and went trick or treating with the goblins.

One day, Mama said to Papa, "The wife of the Minister of Fisheries told me she lives a block from our house, and she kindly invited Ayako to come and play with her daughter, as they are the same age."

"How very nice of her. It's good to have friends in the neighborhood; besides, the Legrands are French Canadians, and there are no French Canadians at Elmwood."

I went for lunch one Saturday. There were only the two of us, as Marie's father was busy and her mother did not join us. We sat in the large, dark dining room and ate an elaborate meal.

"You like to play weez my dolls?" Marie's English was limited and heavily accented.

"Can we play in the garden?" It was a beautiful day and we went out into a courtyard; it was stone-paved with no place for hide and seek. "Want to play tag?"

"No like."

"Oh. How about skipping rope?"

"No. I too tired."

Mme. Legrand came to the doorway. "*Mais, qu'est-ce que tu fais ici? Pourquoi ne joues-tu pas avec tes poupées?*"

"*Elle ne veut pas. Elle est comme un garçon; elle ne sait que jouer a 'tag' et 'skip'*"

"*Bon, bon.*"

I understood the "tag" and "skip" and the complaining tone of voice. The rest was too fast for my French, despite Mme. Hervé's efforts.

Mme. Legrand smiled at me. "Would you like to color some books?"

So we colored, which both of us liked, even if I hated art class at school. We became friends.

"Would you like to come to my party next Saturday?"

"I like."

"Oh good. Two o'clock?"

"Two o'clock? Not finish lunch."

"Three then?"

"Yes."

Marie arrived, beautifully dressed. Frannie, Jean, Estelle, Dot, Laura, and I had been playing hide and seek, and we continued to play, but Marie could not be coaxed to join. She remained serious and quiet and after a while we left her alone.

"I go home."

"But Marie, we've just started. Would you like to see my dolls? Aren't you going to stay for tea?" I wiped my forehead with the back of my hand.

"No. I go home."

"Do you have to?"

No answer. Marie just left.

"What's the matter with her?" asked Frannie.

"Oh well, she's different," I answered.

"Spoilsport."

"She's quite nice. It's just that she doesn't like running around. Maybe we should have played something else."

"Ha."

"I go home," mimicked Laura. Everyone laughed.

Marie and I kept on visiting. We colored, made dresses for dolls, did puzzles, and baked cookies. Cookies were especially fun, for Marie had all shapes of cookie-cutters: stars, crescents, Christmas trees. Sometimes we made gingerbread men.

Our parties, though, were failures. I went to Marie's patron saint's day feast, which started very late, at five. There were a lot of elderly relatives, such as aunts, uncles, and grandparents, and everyone spoke in rapid French. I ate a lot, as there seemed little else to do, and began feeling sick. I wanted to say "I go home" as she had.

Marie came to two more of my parties, where she sulked and left suddenly each time, saying, "I go home."

The girls whispered, "Here comes 'I go home'" when she arrived.

Marie stopped coming to my parties. Then she stopped coming to my house altogether and I stopped going to hers.

Locky became my best friend, along with Frannie. Mama had been persuaded to have a dog again.

"You had a St. Bernard the last time you were here; I remember how Masa loved to play with that dog. Certainly you could have a tiny West Highland White Terrier. It'll be good for Ayako to have a pet around the house," said Mrs. Horwood.

"But we move around so much, and besides, it's so sad when they die like our Scottie in London."

"None of *my* dogs will die of distemper." Mrs. Horwood had a litter of four puppies. "Westies are the ideal pet: not as high-strung as fox terriers nor as stubborn as Scotties. They're cheerfully quiet."

Lockiel, named after Loch Lockiel, arrived when he was two months old and immediately became my best friend. During the winter holidays, Ruby, our fierce-looking cook, spurned me just as Goto had, greeting me with "Get out of my kitchen!" each time I would trespass. Hana had returned to Japan to be married. Katie the maid played with me but had to work hard to make up for lost time, which made me feel guilty. Frannie was away skiing and Estelle was visiting a cousin in Toronto. So it was Locky who romped with me in the snow and skated with me. Whiskers stiffened with balls of snow, he's run onto the rink, slide across, and crash into the snow bank.

"Up, sit up." "Down, lie down." "Give me your paw." Locky was a very obedient dog if a reward of dog biscuits was forthcoming.

With his short legs, he was also a skier with good balance. He would jump onto the back of my skis at the Royal Ottawa Golf Club, waiting to go down the slopes with me.

"Get off, Locky." With no biscuits in sight, he was deaf.

"I'll fall. Get off before I fall!" But most of the time we kept our balance and swooshed down the slopes.

Locky, while not human, was very much alive. I found another friend who was alive only in my imagination.

Once, Papa went to New York on business and Mama accompanied him to buy clothes.

"There's nothing in Ottawa, and this is so much faster than ordering from Paris."

I used to admire the elegant sketches sent from Paris from which Mama chose her good clothes.

Mama returned from New York with a navy evening dress with pleats that flashed scarlet when she walked ("very daring and American"), and Papa had bought her a necklace to match. She had also brought back a number of suits. For me, there was a white party dress with pale pink embroidered flowers.

Papa finally brought out a ten-inch bear carrying a sizeable basket of chocolates.

"I asked the saleslady, 'Could I just have the basket of chocolates without the bear? He's rather bulky for my suitcase.' But she was quite a saleswoman. I wish I had someone like her at the office—young and pretty, too. 'I'm sorry, sir, but this bear's had this basket for a long time and he's quite attached to it. It would be a shame to take it away from him!' So of course, the bear came with the chocolates."

I fell in love with the bear from the moment I saw him. I had lots of bears: big ones, fuzzy ones, musical ones, ones that growled when punched in the stomach, all relegated to the same fate as the rest of my dolls: lined up on shelves in my room, gathering dust. This plain teddy had very short beige hair, brown glass eyes, and a nose and mouth of coarse black thread. He neither growled nor played music, but he had a perky smile, Locky's smile. His eyes and nose and mouth were filled with mischief and he was alive, whereas the other bears were just stuffed toys.

I simply called him "Teddy" and he went with me everywhere. He had his own suitcase, and his wardrobe outdid any Shirley Temple doll's. His little nose had to be sewn on again and again and his face became quite threadbare.

Locky and Teddy accompanied us on our travels. Locky lived till he was eleven and ever since, the Westie has been my favorite breed. After Locky died, Teddy moped in dark corners, until one day he disappeared. Did he go in search of his friend?.

Mama and Papa had guests even more than on Bayswater Road. The straight staircase from the front hall was just right for watching guests as they entered the house. I crouched behind the banisters on the landing, the smell of rosewater from the drawing room wafting up with the perfume of the ladies who removed their wraps in the foyer. Everyone was too busy exchanging greetings to look up until one evening, when pretty young Mrs. Mori of the embassy spotted me.

"Why it's Ayako-san!"

I put my finger to my lips. "Ssh."

A red-haired lady and a hairless man looked up. All three were smiling.

"Is she the daughter?"

"Hello." The red-haired lady waved, so I had to wave back.

"Why, Mr. and Mrs. Johnson, what are you doing out there? Mrs. Mori, why don't you bring them in here?" Mama followed their eyes. "Oh, are you still up?"

"Come downstairs little girl and say hello to us."

"I can't, I'm in my pajamas."

"That doesn't matter."

I went downstairs gingerly and curtseyed in my pajamas.

"My daughter does the same thing."

"Why don't you join us." Four more people had arrived.

"I think I'll go upstairs—I have to go to bed." And with that, I escaped, followed by laughter.

Sometimes I was allowed to join, when films on Japan were shown in the basement: waterfalls, temples, flower arrangement, tea ceremonies—it was all quite dull and not worth being on my best behavior.

When guests came for tea, I was sometimes called in to greet them. One guest stood out vividly because of a lunch with her that Papa had described. Mama had returned to Japan to see Masa soon after coming to Ottawa. After she came back, Papa went to Tokyo for briefings, and on his stopover in Honolulu, he lunched at Doris Duke Cromwell's house on Diamond Head.

"Imagine, Hide, at this Shangri-la, fish were swimming behind the glass walls of the dining room. 'Which would you like for lunch?' she asked. 'Oh, any one, maybe this one, though it's a shame to catch it.' 'That's what they're here for!' After several cocktails, this fish appears for lunch, *meunièred*. 'Delicious,' I say as she eats her salad lunch. 'Really? Let me try.' She reaches over and spears the rest of the fish. 'Mmm, not bad,' she says as I stare at my empty plate."

This fish lady dropped in for tea.

"So, this is your little girl. Hello." She extended a rather bored hand as I curtseyed. She was very beautiful, like a blonde Duchess of Windsor, with thin, long eyebrows and a bright red mouth.

The Japanese Minister was not always popular in 1939. When King George and Queen Elizabeth visited Canada it was a big occasion, and of course, the diplomatic corps was presented at one of the functions. I remember this because Papa came back quietly angry, and I seldom saw him with lips pursed.

"I've never been so insulted in public before." Papa glared at Mama. "We all line up to be presented in turn to their Royal Highnesses, who leisurely exchange pleasantries with everyone as they walk down the line. When they come to us, I say, 'I had the honor of being stationed in your country twice, from 1924 to 1927 and from 1936 to 1938' and bow. King George does not say a word, does not smile, but instead just looks through me and, after a minute, walks on. It was a snub not to me but to Japan and fully meant to be so."

"Now, now," soothed Mama, "the Queen spoke to us, didn't she?"

"But the Queen, who's usually so gracious, snubbed us, too. 'How interesting,' she says in glacial tones as she walks on."

Summertime

In summer I was sent to camp.

"It's a very Canadian and American experience, and she'll love it," Mama was told by friends.

"I don't want to go. I'll hate it. You'll see, I'll hate it."

"We'll see, and if you don't like it you needn't go next summer."

They chose Camp Oconto on Muskoka Lake, as Janet and Jean would be there; it was usual for camps to have Indian names, as they normally taught Indian skills such as canoeing, riding, pottery, and basket-weaving We were to prepare to survive in the wilderness after being coddled at home all winter. I arrived with the required items, which included a formidable amount of mosquito netting to protect our city skins.

"Why do we have this huge square mosquito net?" I asked Jean, who was to be my roommate in our five-room bungalow. Jean was an old hand, as she had come last year.

"Because there's lots of mosquitoes and other bugs."

We sewed looped tapes onto the corners of the nets to hang them from the nails near the ceiling. It was difficult to get it right.

Jean had finished and was standing on her bed, testing the tapes for length. "See, you can peek into Mrs. Schlegel's room from up here." The dividing walls did not go all the way to the top—they stopped five inches from the ceiling, allowing Mrs. Schlegel to hear any whispering after bedtime and spot flashlights from any of the four rooms surrounding her central one. "I can also see a daddy long legs on your mosquito net."

I shrieked and dropped my net. "Is it poisonous?!"

"Don't be silly; they're nothing." Jean flicked it away. "Soon you'll be seeing real spiders—tarantulas, maybe. They come whooshing down when you're asleep and kill you in a second; that's why you need the mosquito net. After you finish with the tapes, better whiten your shoes, because Mrs. Schlegel checks to see whether your shoes are clean when we salute the flag in the morning." We had saddle shoes, white at the tips and back, brown in the middle. I'd have to apply three coatings on the white parts, waiting for each coating to dry before applying the next. I was right to hate camp.

At bedtime, the eight girls in our bungalow filed past Mrs. Schlegel, who was seated at a table in her middle room, spoon in hand. On the table were a bottle, a pitcher of orange juice, and lots of glasses.

"Castor oil, Jennie?"

"No, thank you."

"Castor oil, Beatrice?"

"I don't need it tonight, Mrs. Schlegel."

"Castor oil, Ayako?"

"Why? What's it for?"

"It's to keep you healthy. Cleans out your system. Mix it in orange juice and it tastes delicious."

"I'll try a little bit then."

"That's a good girl; it'll do you good."

I took a sip and made a face, for the mixture tasted like axle grease. The girls were laughing.

"I *love* castor oil," one of them said. "May I have some? And don't mix mine with orange juice, Mrs. Schlegel."

"Oh, you're just showing off," scoffed Jean.

"Fraidy-cat!" Eunice gulped down her castor oil. "Mmmm, it's good."

At breakfast we took turns waiting on tables, and I discovered that the cereal bowls were terribly heavy.

"Ayako, watch out with that tray! Oh, didn't I warn you. You've spilled oatmeal all over my skirt!"

"I'm awfully sorry, Mrs. Schlegel. I didn't mean to."

"Nobody *means* to, but you should have known better than to load the tray like that."

"Your skirt's all dirty!"

"You're telling me. Oh well, never mind, it's washable. But you're to write 'I will be more careful' fifty times."

I gradually discovered the more pleasant side of camping. I learned to swim and canoe and I loved it, mishaps and all. We practiced in big, dark Muskoka Lake, surrounded by pine trees. Miss Connors and Miss Davidson were young and athletic.

"Girls, you can't go canoeing till you know how to swim, so those who can't swim should try hard." I was one of the non-swimmers practicing in our little inlet.

"Ayako, float on your back. I'll hold you up. Relax! I thought all Japanese were good swimmers. What happened to you?" Suddenly, Miss Connors let go of me. I felt something slithering across my forehead as I sank, then I was pulled up, sputtering.

"Sorry I dropped you. A water snake just swam across your forehead and I panicked. Sorry! I'll hold on to you the next time. Are you all right?"

Soon I managed to swim at least well enough to try canoeing. Canoes above our heads, two girls to a canoe, we learned to launch and paddle around our inlet. Even in the shallows, I marveled at the silence and swiftness, the ability to move left or right at just a touch—it was like ice-skating. Before we could venture further, we had to learn to overturn the canoe and right it.

"Hold your breath, go under the canoe, and right it!

The canoe that I maneuvered so lightly was suddenly very heavy, but after much sputtering, laughing, and swimming after our runaway canoe, I got the knack.

"Very good. Now, one girl on each side and climb into the canoe. Spread yourselves over the top instead of just grabbing the sides so the canoe won't tip over. That was wobbly, wasn't it. All right, let's try again."

We had energy to spare, so this was fun and adventure. The really good swimmers and older girls, like Janet, canoed further out in the lake, and Jean and I were taken to watch one of their survival practices in the deep. Fully dressed, they had to jump off their canoe and take off their clothes and shoes in the water. We were deliciously scared and impressed.

Before the camp ended, Jean and I joined a convoy of canoes for a picnic lunch on the other end of the lake.

"Keep near the shore, girls, but not too close, just follow me!" Miss Davidson shouted from her canoe up front. That made six canoes, including Miss Connor's, which was at the rear.

We glided over the water, our paddles hardly making a ripple. It was a beautiful day and we could smell the pine trees. Despite our life jackets, we were all Hiawathas.

Noon saw us transformed into Minnehahas at our destination, gathering wood and cooking to the tune of grumbling stomachs. Never mind that the cooking consisted of heating up cans of baked beans—they never tasted so good. I'd love baked beans and marshmallows forever because they'd always remind me of happiness.

Marshmallows were skewered on sticks on special evenings and toasted over a big fire as we gathered to sing songs and tell stories.

"Row, row, row your boat…"

"Your marshmallows are getting black!"

"Ow, it's hot!"

"You are my sunshine…"

"Oh, that's a stupid song, Miss Davidson!"

"Well then, does anybody know a really scary story?"

At bedtime, I was now expert at crawling into the mosquito net unaccompanied by any insects. I still hated spiders.

"Jean, there are three daddy long legs on my blanket. How did they get into the mosquito net?" Light filtered onto the ceiling from Mrs. Schlegel's lamp.

"Maybe you have a hole."

"I don't."

"Then they came in with you."

"Don't be silly. I always shake myself, shake the net, and take a good look before jumping in."

"I put them in there. Ha, ha!"

"Ayako and Jean, will you be quiet. It's past your bedtime." Mrs. Schlegel was eavesdropping again. Jean crept out of her mosquito net and put her eye to a hole in the wall, one of two tiny holes in the pinewood partition.

"She's knitting."

"What's she knitting?"

"Some awful green socks."

We whispered and giggled, promising to be roommates again next summer before we dropped off to sleep.

I never saw Camp Oconto again, because next summer I toured the Maritime provinces by car with my parents. Digby Pines, Murray Bay, Gaspé Peninsula, St. Andrews, Cape Tormentine, Halifax. Photo albums show us smiling in front of impressive sights, but I remember only minor incidents that could have happened anywhere.

"Papa, I'm awfully thirsty. Can I drink something?"

"It *is* hot and dusty. Jack, if there is a place we can buy a drink, let's stop."

Jack stopped at a rickety country store. We tumbled out and went inside.

"Hmm," said Papa, "here's this new drink, Coca-Cola, even in such a remote place. Has anyone tried it?"

"I have," answered Mr. Imai, Papa's young Japanese-Canadian secretary, who was accompanying us, "but I didn't like it; it tasted like medicine. It's said to contain caffeine and is bad for the health."

"I'm curious. Let's try it," said Papa.

"But if it's bad for your health…" worried Mama.

"It can't be that bad. Let's at least try it once. Yes? Ayako, maybe you'd like lemonade? No, you want Coca-Cola too? Jack? Yes? Mr. Imai, maybe you'd prefer lemonade? Yes?"

I had never drunk anything as delicious as this new drink: bubbly and cold and sweet, a bit like licorice. "I *like* this Coca-Cola!"

We lost our way leaving the port city of Halifax. This was not difficult, as Jack had two pet hates: being passed by other cars and asking for directions.

Papa finally said, "Jack, why don't you ask that driver who's been following us for the last hour how to get out of this park and out of Halifax? I'm sure he's going our way."

Jack stopped and flagged down a navy blue car with a military man behind the wheel. "Could you tell me, sir, how to get to the south exit of this town?"

"Why, what a coincidence. I was just going there myself. Follow me."

We waved him goodbye at the outskirts and a brown car tailed us after that for a while.

"Why are we being followed, Papa?"

"There are lots of ships and navy installations here."

"How exciting to be followed. How could you tell?"

"He was an amateur. I think it's sad that is has come to this."

Digby Pines, Murray Bay, Gaspé Peninsula, St. Andrews, Cape Tormentine, Halifax. I remembered all this as "the trip where we tried Coca-Cola and were followed by two cars."

Last Months in Canada

"We're going back to Japan, Ayako," Papa said late in the summer of 1940. "It will be good to see Masa again, won't it?"

Of course I was happy to be reuniting with Masa, but I felt guilty that I was sadder at leaving Frannie and Jean and Estelle and Janet and Dot and Laura and school...

"Can we take Locky?"

"Yes," said Mama, "we'll be frowned upon for taking back a dog when life is grim now back home, but we'll have to take Locky—he's one of the family."

Before we left, the new American magazine *Life* wanted a photograph of Papa for an article on Japanese diplomats. He had one taken by Yousouf Karsh as a memento of his stay in Canada.

"He certainly knows how to pose his subjects. Talks to them, makes them relax and then snap, snap, snap."

Whatever Karsh's way, that became my favorite photo of Papa, sitting at his desk with a twinkle in his eyes.

"Before we leave, I would like to pay my respects to Mr. Mackenzie King," said Papa. "He was very kind to me when I was a lowly secretary and has continued to be a friend for old times' sake. Considering the world situation, I especially appreciate it."

"A gentleman of the old school, isn't he?" said Mama. "You'd never guess he was the grand old man of the political world here."

"Of course," Papa said, laughing. "By 'old times' sake' he's always under the delusion that we studied at the University of Chicago at the same time. I kept telling him I never went to the University of Chicago, but he's never accepted that and insists on introducing me as 'My old friend Shu Tomii. We were together at the University of Chicago.' He must have me mixed up with some Chinese scholar; I'm quite a bit younger than he is, too. Anyhow, I've given up explaining that he's mixing me up with someone else; if he wants to think I have a degree from the University of Chicago, I could do worse."

"You are impossible."

I accompanied Papa and Mama to Kingsmere, Mr. Mackenzie King's country house. It was a large, comfortable house with a big fire roaring in the drawing room.

The host came forward with tweedy, outstretched arms. "My good friend! And Baroness Tomii! And what is this young lady's name? He bent down and beamed, eyes twinkling beneath bushy eyebrows.

"Ayako." As I curtseyed, I spotted an Airedale hobbling down the stairs. "May I pet your dog?"

Mr. Mackenzie King came with me to the dog, who lay down, thumping his tail. "I suppose it's all right. You see, he's very old, like me, so sometimes he's cranky." We both patted his head.

"How old is he?"

"Sixteen, and he just lost his great friend, who was seventeen, so he's very sad."

"Sixteen! That's very old. Our West Highland White Terrier is a year and a half."

"Then he still has many years to enjoy with you."

After tea, we walked the extensive grounds of Kingsmere, the host waving his cane to point out the sights. I gazed at the large tombstone of the Airedale, ready for him next to an identical one where his seventeen-year-old friend was buried.

"Why does he have a grave when he's still alive?"

"There are so many uncertain things is the world, little girl, that I'm sure he's happy knowing he'll be lying next to his old friend."

Mr. Mackenzie King and Papa shook hands for a long time.

"We have a saying in Japan: 'What happens twice happens thrice.' Our paths crossed in the twenties and again in the thirties. I hope they will cross a third time."

"Perhaps we'll meet again; one never knows. If I were younger I'd say we'll meet again many, many years from now. Goodbye, and take care of yourself."

"Goodbye, and thank you."

"And anyway, our paths have crossed three times already. Remember the University of Chicago?"

We were given a big welcome by the Japanese-Canadians in Vancouver. Salmon fishing, Butchart Gardens, and invitations to homes were crammed into the few days before we sailed.

There were a lot of speeches: "Baron Tomii, we wish to thank you for all you have done for us. We're sorry you are leaving us."

"I'm sorry to be leaving, too, because I have accomplished so little. I realize the difficulties facing the Japanese-Canadians, especially in the fishing industry, just as the Japanese-Americans are struggling in the agricultural industry in California. We need legislation, but it's going to be a slow process requiring education and better communication on both sides. Everyone has to help, so please continue your efforts, integrate where possible, and don't lose heart: your hardships will pave the way towards a better world for your children and grandchildren."

In the early 1960s, I revisited Canada, where I had spent the most carefree years of my childhood. One ninety-two Daly Avenue belonged to some Catholic Brothers and looked the worse for wear. Elmwood School and its grounds seemed smaller than I remembered but was thriving. Laura's home was now the residence of the Japanese Ambassador. Michael Browning had remarried, and after she became widowed, Mrs. Browning found the house too large. Laura had married and moved to Vancouver. Frannie and Estelle had also married and were living elsewhere. I visited Janet. She was a wife, mother, and teacher and lived in a beautiful, modern little house; she had changed little and was still the thoroughly nice, sporty friend of my childhood. We keep in touch, and someday I hope to get to Ottawa again to see her. Frannie moved from wide-open space to wide-open space with her family, possibly for the four or five huge dalmatians she keeps. Now she lives in Calgary and is a judge in dog shows. Her husband, in his letters, told me all this, for Frannie is a terrible correspondent.

JAPAN

The Higashi Nakano House
and
Keimei School

In October 1940 we settled in our house in Higashi-Nakano. It was smaller than the Yakuohji place, meaning less work for Grandmother and an easy commute for Masa to Seikei School, as the train station was only a seven-minute walk from home. I did not become attached to the house, as we were there for so short a period, but then, it had also been a short period at beloved Yakuohji. Perhaps it was the unease and watchfulness in the air because of *hijohji*, "extraordinary times," or more simply, the "crisis." *Hijohji* was a word that I often heard on the radio and wherever I went in Tokyo. Caution seeped into even the walls of our home. Life was no longer so carefree.

Grandmother spent the better part of the day in her room smoking and staring at the garden or meditating in front of an altar to Grandfather. Cousin Setsuko had just married a banker and had a home of her own.

Occasionally, Masa would practice his judo on me.

"Ouch!" I would cry as I fell to the *tatami* mat. "Why do I always have to be the one thrown?"

"You have to learn to fall well before you can throw. But all right, I'll teach you a few tricks."

It was fun. I wished I could try my judo on Frannie—and what would Marie say if she could see me now! But most of the time, Masa was at school or doing homework or playing with his own friends.

Father worked long hours and entertained outside the house. Mother, as the eldest son's wife, had many family matters to take care of, and she also visited the Nakamuras, her side of the family.

The maids were busy in the kitchen, which was large but crammed with gas rings, braziers, and dangerous paraphernalia to cook bland but exotic dishes that were not appetizing to watch being made.

"What kind of soup are you making, Kiku?"

"This is soybean soup, *ojohsama*. I don't think you've seen this kind abroad."
Kiku placed chunks of tofu in the warm soup. She reached into a basket of
squirming loaches and threw them in, then turned on the gas.

"What are you doing? How awful."

"You're sometimes served soybean soup with tofu and loaches, aren't you?
This is how you make it."

"I hate it. I always leave it."

"It's very nutritious, and your grandmother loves it. This is how you get the
loaches inside the tofu. The tofu is still cold and the soup is warm but not boiling. To escape from the heat, the loaches swim into the tofu, then we boil the
whole thing. After turning off the gas, we add soybean paste."

I peered into the soup in fascination and horror. Dark worm-like creatures
squirmed and disappeared into the white tofu. One loach didn't make it before
the water reached the boil and floated belly-up. Kiku picked him up with chopsticks and put him aside.

"This one doesn't go to the dining room."

"How can they disappear if they're so long?"

"They curl up inside."

"I think it's *awful*. I'm so glad I never eat it."

"It's delicious. And they're only loaches," chimed in Hatsu.

The kitchen lost its luster for me. Anyway, *ojohsama* were not supposed to loi-
ter there.

In the cupboard of the dining room, an old radio, the shape and size of an oval
tombstone, sat on a shelf. At 7:00 P.M., the cupboard door was slid open and we
sat around, listening to the evening news:

"A quiet moment for soldiers in China as they read letters from home…Secre-
tary of State Cordell Hull criticizes Japan again…In Washington, the Japanese
Ambassador called on President Roosevelt…Meanwhile, in Europe, Adolf Hitler…"

Sometimes, father and mother tuned into the forbidden shortwave radio that
they kept hidden in a cupboard of their room, which I shared.

Representatives of the local housewives' association called on mother. They
wore pantaloons and white coverall aprons. "We'd like your cooperation in
Japan's war efforts against China. Our men are dying for their country in a foreign land while we live in comfort here. We are starting a movement to live as
frugally as possible—it's *hijohji*, 'extreme times,' and extreme times require
extreme measures."

"Yes," said mother.

"We are also asking each household to prepare relief packages for the boys on the front. We're giving out these bags, which you can fill with cans of food, caramels, cigarettes, or sweaters knit with all your love. Attach a letter to each bag. We would like you to assemble fifteen bags."

"All right. By when do you want them?"

"In three weeks, to catch a special ship."

"I'll get busy."

"Please do so. Long live the Emperor!"

There were a lot of people in uniform on the streets and among our relatives, too. Uncle Takeo was someplace in China, and cousin Makoto, wearing a smart new uniform, was training to follow in his father's footsteps. Two of mother's brothers were in the navy.

People were tense: *hijohji, hijohji*, I heard all around me. You dared not speak in English or read English books in public, because that was unpatriotic in *hijohji* times.

At Keimei Gakuen I found my familiar child's world. It was a special school for children who had lived abroad and covered first grade through junior high.

"There's a new school just for you," said mother. "Baron Mitsui started it for his two children who lived in England and who need to catch up on Japanese studies."

The Mitsuis had been unable to find a school that met their requirements, so they decided to start their own, offering their beautiful home and garden at Akasaka Daimachi to seventeen students and an equal number of instructors. The Mitsuis themselves came to assemblies and all school events and were surprisingly fast sprinters on Sports Day. We were one big family.

I'd take the train from Higashi Nakano, carrying my black satchel and fifty *sen* emergency money in my pass case. At Shinanomachi I transferred to a tram. It was all very different from being driven to Elmwood School, but it was fun, as I often met my classmate Yuriko on the tram. We played games, often word games.

"Re-be mem-be ber-be not-be to-be speak-be En-be glish-be"

"This-be is-be not-be En-be glish-be. This-be is-be our-be se-be cret-be lan-be guage-be."

"We-be must-be care-be ful-be."

One morning, a soldier standing near us glared and suddenly burst out, "What gibberish are you talking!"

"It's our own language, which we made up."

"Your own language is Japanese *bakayaro*, you idiots! You should be speaking in Japanese! What school do you go to?" The others on the tram pretended not to hear. We were shocked into silence.

"What stupid school do you go to? Don't they teach you anything!"

Fortunately it was our stop next, and we scampered off as the tram bore him away, still shouting invectives.

By azalea season I had only one more month at Keimei Gakuin, because I would be leaving in the middle of the summer for Buenos Aires. The last weeks seemed especially sweet.

"Come and sip honey from these flowers." Azalea bushes abounded at school and Yori taught me to suck the stem of the blossoms, for candies were a luxury by 1941.

"Ayako, can you land a somersault from the parallel bar?" Tomoko did a perfect somersault and landed on her feet. I followed with less grace but landed in one piece in the sand pit.

"Say 'pig' in French, Tomoko. Can you say it in German, Ayako? I can say 'pig' in Italian and Spanish." Yukiko had lived in Rome and knew that Tomoko had returned from Paris and that I had been born in Berlin.

"Did you hear about Akira, that he fainted in zoology class when Mr. Kasai slit open a chicken's stomach? Nobody thought that jokester was afraid of blood."

"Yori's sweet on you!"

"C'mon, kiss her, Yori."

"*You're* sweet on Yukiko, why don't you kiss *her*!"

"No, no."

"Yes, yes."

"Children, enough of this nonsense. Mr. Kamijo is waiting to give you your calligraphy lesson."

Classes were small and ages were mixed, with each student given individual attention.

"Not calligraphy!" we moaned, for Mr. Kamijo, a nationally famous calligrapher, hoped in vain that we would live up to his standards. He wasted his time with us as a personal favor to the Mitsuis. Wearing *haori-hakama,* the formal Japanese man's attire, he had a fierce gleam in his eye and his mustache looked like one of his calligraphy brushes. Not only did we write poorly, we sometimes spattered ink on the white walls.

"Draw this horizontal line ten times; it's basic to all Japanese characters. No, no, this is dreadful. Ten more times. All right, I guess you can't do any better today. We'll leave the horizontal line and go on to the vertical line. Hold your brush straight and draw this vertical line ten times." He demonstrated with a powerful black stroke. "Try not to waver or flourish so much, as it shows a lack of control, of concentration, a laxness of spirit, and you can write nothing well until your spirit is disciplined."

I rather enjoyed the calligraphy sessions, though I would have died before admitting that to anyone. It was satisfying to make thin strokes, thick strokes, pressed points, flipped points, quick strokes, and steady ones with a bulge at the end. Control, concentration, he had said. Despite his fierce looks, I admired Mr. Kamijo for his dedication and devotion.

The girls' favorite teacher was Miss Abe. Tall, young, and pretty, she wore bright clothes and painted her nails despite *hijohji*. She taught English and had been brought up in America.

In June, at assembly, Mr. Mitsui looked very grave. "You will all be sorry to hear that two of our most dedicated teachers will be leaving us at the end of the term."

"Who? Miss Abe must be getting married," we whispered.

"Mr. Shoji and Mr. Taira have been drafted into the army. We will miss them sorely, but they will be fighting for our country, so let's give them a big hand. We'll be waiting for you to come back soon!"

"Mr. Shoji?! Mr. Taira?!" Stunned, we clapped as the two stepped up front, faced us, and bowed. Mr. Taira's ruddy face was ruddier than usual; he was blushing. It was hard to believe that Mr. Shoji and Mr. Taira, who had taught me the day before, would be fighting as soldiers. I would not be the only one leaving.

The Kutsukake Mountains,
Before We Leave for Argentina

I left Keimei in less than six months because we were on the move again.

"Not nearly enough time to have learned to read and write like a proper Japanese girl," Grandmother Tomii said with disapproval.

Soon after settling at Higashi-Nakano, father had asked, "Ayako, what would you think about living abroad again?"

"Where?" I had felt an air of excitement in the house.

"Argentina."

"Where's that?"

"Look at your map; it's the other side of the globe. Here's a book about Argentina. It's in Japanese, so you may not be able to read it, but there are a lot of pictures."

The cover showed a man standing by a horse on a prairie. He wore pantaloons and a neckerchief and was holding something gourd-like, from which he sipped with a silver straw. "When?"

"I'll be sailing in February, and you and Mama will come later, as there's still a lot to do before moving house."

"And Masa?"

"I'm afraid we'll have to leave him again." Mother sighed. "That's what weighs on my heart, especially considering this uncertain world situation. Argentina is so far, literally the other end of the earth."

"Poor boy. I wish we could all stay together, especially in these threatening times, but when you think of his future, we can't take him with us. He'd be an outsider after he came back, never accepted, neither fish nor fowl, as I often say, unhappy like Tatsuo Kuwabara's poor son. Masa knew we'd be leaving again but didn't expect it to happen this soon. It was unfortunate."

"I hate this moving around, having to speak in different languages and not having a private life. I'd really like a quiet life in Japan in a little house with garden and both children with us."

Father made appeasing sounds, but I was quite surprised. The Mama I knew until these days of *hijohji* was always beautifully dressed and perfumed. She went to parties, gave parties, went shopping, and spent less time with me, it seemed, than Papa did. She seemed happy. I couldn't imagine her wanting to stay at home and putter about the garden. It was only after father retired that other aspects of my mother revealed themselves. In her old age, I crowned her as the perfect mother.

Father sailed in February 1941 on the SS *Tatsuta Maru* for San Francisco, then he took another ship from New York to Buenos Aires, as ambassador to Argentina and minister to Uruguay and Paraguay. It was his first posting outside of North America and Europe, and he spent the last months reading up on Latin America, talking to "old hands," and studying the general political situation. He loved his work and enjoyed living in different countries; he saw his first posting in a Latin-American country as a challenge. There was a sparkle in his eyes.

After Keimei, I joined Grandmother Nakamura at her summer cottage up in the mountains of Sengataki, in Kutsukake, near Karuizawa. I would commune with nature, be kept from underfoot as mother made final preparations, and also get to know my other grandmother better.

Grandmother Nakamura was very different from Grandmother Tomii, who was quiet, stubborn, and dignified, seated on her cushion at Higashi-Nakano, eyes closed, rosary in hand, meditating with lips pursed or praying for Grandfather. She was every inch a lady. Grandmother Nakamura was just as old and just as stubborn, and much richer, but she could never sit still. During the summer she climbed to the top of volcanic Mt. Asama, went Asama berry picking, made Asama berry juice and jam, pickled plums, visited hot springs for her health, where she swallowed foul-smelling sulfurous water, changed from kimono to kimono to visit friends, and loved to entertain.

Grandmother Tomii agreed with Miss Temple of Frances Holland that "it is vulgar to discuss food" and rarely entered the kitchen. "Ladies do not wander into the kitchen." Bland fare was served, forcing Grandfather Tomii to go to restaurants for more exotic dishes.

Grandmother Nakamura talked a lot about food, often took part in the final stages of cooking a meal, and served a variety of well-seasoned, spicy Chinese dishes in addition to the bland fare that I had come to expect.

Grandmother had several cottages in her compound, and she lived in the small one with the tricky bathtub. This round cauldron was made of metal, and you had to balance on a board in its black depths if you didn't want to burn your feet. Without the proper balance, the board popped up and clipped you on the chin. I thought of pictures of explorers boiling in huge pots tended by cannibals.

"Ouch! The board's popped up to my shoulders again and my toes are cooking, Grandma!"

"Just push it under your feet."

"Why do you have this kettle-like bathtub?"

"Cauldron, you mean. Because we are in the country, without modern conveniences, and water boils faster in this kind of tub. If you're afraid of this, what are you going to do when Mt. Asama erupts?"

"When is it going to erupt?"

"There are little eruptions all the time. Years ago, during the big eruption, lava flowed down like a river of fire and melted everything in its path. The dried-up lava is where we went to pick the Asama berries."

"What if it erupts while you're climbing, Grandma?"

"Well, then it will be goodbye Grandma, ha ha ha."

Mt. Asama did erupt during the summer. A distant "boom" was followed by falling ashes, which kept the maids busy wiping the house. Grandmother said, "Just ashes this time. I remember a few years ago when pebbles, almost stones, came pelting down."

About the only time Grandmother sat down, aside from when she was eating, was when she smoked her *kiseru* pipe. Only a teaspoonful of tobacco fit into her small, long pipe, similar to an opium pipe and made of silver. She was a heavy smoker, so I'd often hear "Puff, puff," then "clonk, clonk" as she knocked out the remainder of the tobacco, followed by silence as she stuffed a new batch and lit it with charcoal from the brazier, then it started again: "puff, puff", "clonk, clonk", silence, an occasional cough. She produced quite a rhythm.

I rolled toilet tissues into pipe stem lengths, lit them with charcoal from the brazier, and puffed, but they did not taste good.

Masa joined us later, in Kutsukake, and mother came up twice. Masa had become much nicer than in his water-pistol days, and we roamed beyond the compound, butterfly hunting together.

"You've caught a moth, Ayako."

"But this is too pretty to be a moth. It must be a butterfly!"

"No matter how pretty, if it tucks its wings back in a triangle when it perches, it's a moth. Butterflies, when they perch, fold their wings upwards."

There were hundreds of butterflies: white, green, spotted, striped, leaf-shaped, small ones, and huge ones. Later on there were dragonflies, some caramel-colored, others red with gauze wings that we grasped with our fingers.

"I like the large blue butterflies but most of all the big black ones with the light green stripes."

"Some come around here, but you'll find lots more deeper in the mountains. I'll take you there this afternoon."

At 2:00 P.M., butterfly net in hand, piqué hat on my head, thermos dangling from a shoulder strap, I waited on my bicycle. Masa had two nets, and next to his flask dangled a butterfly cage and a triangular butterfly tin. The tin contained a syringe, a vial of alcohol, and wax paper.

"We'll get off our bicycles after ten minutes and walk a little. You'll see lots of the ones you like, usually in pairs. Wait till it perches before you catch it so as not to damage the wings."

I caught two large blue ones, though the striped ones escaped, one with a torn wing.

"You have to be more careful. That butterfly's going to die."

"It'll die anyway, if I catch it."

"But then you can preserve and enjoy it. This way it'll be eaten up by ants."

"Here's two more of these blue ones!"

"Leave them alone; we already have two of those. I'll show you what to do with the ones we caught." He folded their wings and thrust an alcohol-filled syringe into their bodies. They stopped struggling.

"Ugh."

"You don't want them to struggle and have all the powder come off the wings."

That evening, we unfolded the wings and pinned them onto boards, left wing to left board, right wing to right board, with the torso dangling between the boards.

"I don't like this part of catching butterflies."

"Cruel, isn't it, but you don't want to catch them just to throw them away, do you? I free most, keeping only new ones for my collection."

Too soon the weeks passed by, and we returned to Tokyo in late August to say goodbye and part again, to be separated by half the globe.

Masa sulked. "I always have to stay behind. Ayako goes—even Locky goes."

"You know that—" started mother.

"Yes, I know, boys need a Japanese education to be accepted into Japanese society later on…but I don't have to like it."

"Besides, you will be a joy to your grandmother."

"Mmm-hmm."

"Your Uncle Yujiro and your Aunt Ruriko will be staying at our house again. Perhaps we could arrange to have you take a year off and visit us; and anyway, we'll only be away about two years."

"Girls are lucky."

During the big air raid of May 25, 1945, much of Tokyo inside the Yamanote line was destroyed, including our Higashi-Nakano house. Nobody was there to put out the approaching fires: my grandmother had died, Uncle Yujiro and Aunt Ruriko had moved out of the city, and Masa was boarding at the engineering department of Tokyo University across the bay before entering the draft. The house next door and those to the left remained intact.

Keimei also burned during air raids, but there were no casualties, as the school had already moved to the Mitsuis' Haijima house on the outskirts of Tokyo. After the war, Mr. Shoji became headmaster of this relocated Keimei, with its huge rolling grounds near a river. Mr. Taira was killed in action. Mr. and Mrs. Mitsui devoted themselves to the school till they passed away a few years ago, and now that there is no dormitory, Keimei has more local students than returnees.

Part of the stone wall remains from Grandmother Nakamura's Kutsukake compound, which has been split up into summer cottages and company villas, perhaps owned by the empire built by a clerk in the local ward office in my grandmother's days. His name was Tsutsumi

Ayako and Locky in garden. 192 Daly Avenue, Ottawa, 1938.

Baroness Hide Tomii, Janet, Ayako. Camp Oconto, Ontario, 1938.

Baron Tomii with Mr. MacKenzie-King. Kingsmere, 1939.

Baroness Tomii, Ayako with Locky, Baron Tomii, Masahide Tomii. The
Higashi Nakano house, Tokyo, 1940.

ARGENTINA

The Journey

"A typhoon is approaching. Please return inside."

Mother looked at the calm sea and at the steward. We were a day out of Yokohama and were enjoying the sea air on our deck chairs.

"All right. But it's rather early for a typhoon, isn't it?"

"Yes, ma'am, typhoon season is usually September, but they seem to like the sea around Japan."

It was so peaceful, and there was nobody else around, so we stayed another five minutes. As we gathered our blankets, the seas suddenly became rough. The ship tilted and we slid to the edge of the deck. Mother grabbed me and the railing.

"Hold on to me and go for that door!"

I was quite scared, but as the ship soared on another wave then tilted in the opposite direction, we almost made it to the door before we stumbled backwards again.

"Help! Someone please help us!" Mother shouted loudly as we flattened ourselves on the deck. The purser stepped out quickly, dragged us inside, and bolted the door.

"You should have been warned to come inside!"

"We were, but I never thought it would come so soon. The sea was so calm!"

"You should never underestimate the speed of a typhoon; you could have been swept overboard. The sea can change in minutes."

"I'm sorry for causing you so much trouble. I'll know better the next time."

The ship was tossed about for two days. A steward tied the drawers and cupboards in our cabin after we took out what we needed. At mealtimes, holding on to the railing in the corridors, we weaved our way to the dining room, where I saw from the large windows how the ship rolled left, on a swell, then right, on a swell, then left again. This must be what a roller coaster was like; it was very exciting. The tables were chained to the floor, the tablecloths were dampened to prevent chinaware and glasses from slipping, one waiter lost his balance with a full tray. The dining room was nearly empty and became emptier as the meal progressed. Mother and I, both seaworthy, had healthy appetites, and so did Mr. Ninomiya, who sat at the captain's table with us, but his wife was less hardy.

Mr. Ninomiya shook his head. "My wife insists that we get off at Hawaii and return to Japan. She says it will kill her to stay on the ship till San Francisco. She says she'd rather die than spend two weeks on board for the return voyage."

"But you were both looking forward to seeing your new grandson!"

"We were, but Mitsuko never imagined the voyage would be like this, and she absolutely refuses to go further. I'm afraid we'll have to turn back. She looks terrible."

The seas were calm after that, and it was to be quite a long voyage, as we planned to stay on the same ship from Yokohama to Buenos Aires, unlike father. From San Francisco, we sailed towards the Panama Canal without the Ninomiyas, who had gotten off at Honolulu as they said they would. Going through the Panama Canal would be a very interesting experience, said mother.

While we were having dinner one evening, I found *hijohji* followed us here, too.

The captain laid down his napkin and stood up. He cleared his throat and looked uncomfortable. "I'm afraid, ladies and gentlemen, we won't be able to go through the Panama Canal. We have just been informed that no Japanese ships will be allowed from now on."

There was a buzz and voices of consternation.

"Oh dear."

"What shall we do?"

"I told you we should have sailed on an earlier ship"

"What are you going to do, captain?"

"Are you going to turn back?"

"I'll shortly be distributing a more detailed announcement to all the passengers, but I have decided after much thought and consultation to press on to Argentina and Brazil through the Straits of Magellan. We won't be passing through in summer, but if Magellan could do it, I should be able to do it on a modern ship."

"But that's terribly dangerous!"

"Supposing we hit an iceberg!"

"It'll take so long!"

"I'm sorry to cause you all this inconvenience, but we've come this far, and it's the only way we can get you to your destinations. It would be easy to turn back, but that would upset all your plans. I will take every precaution, waiting near the straits till conditions are good; so yes, it may take quite a while."

It was *hijohji*—meals became simple and water was rationed till we reached Lima. We could not go through the Panama Canal because of tense relations with the U.S., mother told me, but what did all this mean? I did not understand. Later tensions made this the last passenger ship to sail to this hemisphere from Japan before World War II.

Father telegraphed that mother and I should get off at Valparaiso in Chile and fly over the Andes in one of those new passenger airplanes. He wanted to see us soon and he was always eager to try new things. Cook and his wife elected to continue by ship. ("No dangerous flying for us, *okusama*. We'll choose the Magellan Straits any time.") So we left Locky with them.

The Japanese minister to Santiago and Mrs. Itoh met us at Valparaiso, where we had delicious shrimps before heading to the legation in the capital.

"Please stay with us as long as you wish. Wait till a really fine day to fly, a day that's clear and without much wind. I must say, you are very brave to travel by airplane, especially over the Andes range. The Aconcagua of the Andes here is the highest mountain in South America, you know."

"Oh? I didn't know that, but I'm sure my husband wouldn't have suggested we fly if it wasn't safe. He said to take Panagra Airlines."

"Of course it must be safe, especially the American airlines Panagra which only flies in clear weather, because Americans are very strict about safety. It alternates days with the other airline, the German Condor, which has a more dependable schedule but is more daring with the weather and has had a few unfortunate incidents. I was just thinking of the inconvenience, as it's still a new thing. The amount of luggage you can take is very limited, and they weigh each passenger, too."

"Perhaps we should have continued by ship if planes aren't reliable, especially as I have my daughter with me."

"No, no, there's nothing to worry about. In fact, it will be much more of an ordeal going through the Magellan Straits, where the seas can be very rough. Also, there's a lot to see in Santiago; we shall be happy to take you both sightseeing and would like you to stay with us as long as you wish."

A Panagra flight was scheduled for two days later and fortunately, there wasn't a cloud in the sky. The plane was full with some twenty-five passengers, and as I was light we were allowed a little extra luggage. We thanked the Itohs and were off.

"Aren't the snow-capped mountains beautiful," said mother.

"Look, Mama, I can see cars driving up that mountain! There are people waving to us!"

"So they are. Whew, I'm beginning to feel short of breath, though we seem to be flying low. I think I'll try this oxygen mask. The stewardess said to use it when we had trouble breathing. How are you?"

"I'm all right, but I think I'll try one of these dangling masks, because they're so funny." After receiving help from the stewardess, we looked like monsters, and I soon took my mask off, feeling no need for the uncomfortable thing.

There was a sharp, jerky movement and the plane plunged downwards, climbed up again, then plunged again. I gripped the arms of my seat as my tummy flip-flopped.

"Ladies and gentlemen, the turbulence is due to air-pockets and is a normal occurrence at such a high altitude. Please check that your seatbelts are secure."

I could see mules pulling a wagon below.

"We are now approaching Mt. Aconcagua, 22,835 feet above sea level. Watch for the *Cristo de los Andes,* the large statue of Christ to your left. Once we pass that, we will be in Argentina."

More downward plunges—the typhoon was much better than this. Were we going to crash? Everyone seemed calm (although some were using sick bags), so I decided we were safe.

"Look, Ayako, there below!" And there, quite clearly, was the statue of Christ, with outstretched arms at the highest point of all those mountains, a lone figure looking out over miles and miles of white snow and blue sky.

Time dragged after that. "Mama, Argentina's a very flat country, isn't it," I said as we passed stretch after stretch of green and brown *pampa* prairies.

What a joy to see father at last at the airport! "Papa!"

Tall, strong, and smiling, Papa's eyes were full of joy as well as he greeted us, but we were all on our best, most restrained behavior, as there were embassy ladies welcoming mother with bouquets of flowers.

Arribeños 1499

In Buenos Aires, many streets are named after important national dates, a boon to history classes: 25 de mayo, 9 de julio. Another help for students worldwide is the penchant for naming streets after important personages.

The embassy residence covered half a block and was defined in the front by Arribeños, at the back by Luis Maria Campos, and on one side by Loreto, streets named after illustrious men. By a happy coincidence, the house number 1499 was the year cited in some history books when Columbus discovered South America. For me, "Arribeños 1499" in residential Belgrano became an address easy to remember.

The house was approached through tall wrought-iron gates, then a driveway that encircled a lawn, with two Japanese stone lanterns that lit up at night. To the right of the driveway was a clay tennis court, hidden by eucalyptus and mimosa. Further towards the rear garden, to the right of the house, was a high-wired pen suitable for a doberman (I kept my rabbit there); a gazebo covered with the branches of lemon trees; and my playground, which included a swing set, parallel bars, and a sandpit; and a small putting green. To the left of the house, where cars drove by on grand party nights on their way out through the rear garden, the grounds formed three balconies overhanging Loreto. As the departing guests wound their way downhill through the floodlit rear garden, they passed a larger gazebo covered with jasmine, a grotto with a pond in front that fed a waterfall that led to another pond, and a Japanese bridge. All this as they drove past eucalyptus trees, palm trees, orange trees, grapefruit trees, camphor trees, a bamboo grove, and of course, the nut trees that the builder and previous owner of the place had planted on the birth days of each of his eight children. The *teru teru* guard birds, long-legged gray birds that cried "teru teru" loudly when strangers approached, might distract the visitors from the mundane gardener's house and garage to the right as they exited through the Louis Maria Campos gates.

The residence itself was classical on the outside, of white stone like the house in San Francisco but on a much grander scale. Inside, there was much wood paneling downstairs, but it was otherwise bare, waiting for my mother to furnish it.

"This house needs to be furnished properly to bring out its beauty. Since the budget won't cover that, I'll try to give the downstairs rooms, at least, a feel of the grand style." Mother's decorating instincts were aroused.

"This wood-paneled room to the left of the entrance should be the small drawing room." This, opposite the cloak room, became the gentlemen's parlor, or blue parlor, an English-style room with a walnut desk, coffee table, comfortable walnut chairs in French blue needlepoint, a deep sofa, and a carpet in French blue and beige.

"Now this can be the general drawing room and on grand occasions become the banquet room," she said, indicating the huge medieval hall in the center of the ground floor, with a large fireplace in the middle and a Steinway in an alcove. It became an austere, dignified drawing room that could on grand occasions give way to a long table, with glittering settings for fifty. Such occasions would be for top Argentine officials, as my parents kept a low profile after Japan went to war. Portraying a nation's austerity and power simultaneously was a delicate balancing act.

"The dining room also has beautiful wood-paneling. I like the bow window facing the rear garden and the side windows, which lighten up the room. English style and a lot of red would go well. And here's the pantry, with a dumb waiter going down to the kitchen."

Mother looked at three whitish connected rooms, two off a larger central one. "The large room can be used to entertain ladies, with Louis XIV gilt chairs and tables." She selected an old rose and beige carpet. One of the smaller rooms was decorated in the same manner, and the other became a game room, with two tables that were used for bridge and mahjong.

"I like this sun room best—look at the huge bay windows and the glass doors leading out to the terrace. Let's have rattan furniture here. Maybe green and white. And plants." This cheerful place became our family room, where good friends joined us.

Paintings arrived later in safety, along with the cook and his wife and Locky. The captain had indeed been cautious and taken his time. Father had selected Japanese artists, including Yokoyama Taikan, Foujita Tsuguji, and Uemura Shoen, and my parents took pleasure in deciding the best spot for each painting.

No interior decorator was consulted; my mother did it all, with father as adviser, and the result was harmonious and beautiful.

"When did you learn to decorate?" complimented my father.

"I'm bad with languages, but I'm fond of lovely clothes and lovely interiors. I've learned by keeping my eyes open at the many beautiful houses we've visited. Even awful ones teach a lesson."

"You've done a professional job."

"Oh, come on, I can't hope to imitate the gorgeous places we've seen, but I thought I might give the feel of style."

"With great success, I must say."

Upstairs there seemed to be a lot of pillared balconies and stained-glass skylights. The rooms exited onto a large central hallway, which had a big round table and chairs, where my mother decided menus with Takada, the cook. A large frosted skylight flooded the hallway with light.

The rooms to the left of this hallway began with the guests' suite and a door that opened onto the back stairs, then came a breakfast room opening onto a balcony. Next, a short corridor led to my father's study. On the way, there was a bathroom with a stained glass skylight that dappled the tiles with myriad colors.

Opposite this corridor, at the end of the right side of the big hallway, was my parents' large, sprawling bedroom with its compartmentalized bathroom and small corner room where my father kept his private safe. A large pillared circular balcony joined the bedroom to my mother's dressing room, where she also kept a bed for naps.

The area nearest the stairs on the right of the big hallway was taken up by my quarters. They consisted of a spacious all-purpose bedroom with a Juliet balcony and a large bathroom accessible by a short corridor. It was the first time I saw a bidet, and to my mother's disgust, I found it just the right size for Locky's bath. As I lay in bed in my room, a eucalyptus tree beyond one window hid the view of the Barreto house on the other half of our block, while a trimmer palm tree outside another window allowed me to see beyond, into our rear garden. The huge eucalyptus tree swayed and rustled in the wind. I grew to love the sound.

Mother decorated the upstairs simply. Also simply though comfortably furnished were a billiard room and a snack-relaxation room in the basement, used by embassy people. Mother let the cook and his wife have most of the say for the kitchen and the staff dining room. The staff living quarters were functionally decorated according to individual wishes, and the workrooms basically were left as they were. I was always eager to make friends with the downstairs staff and was curious about their lives, but for the first time, I was stymied by language. Cook Takada and his wife were the only ones downstairs who understood Japanese, and they regarded me with a cold eye and repelled all my overtures. The others understood only Spanish and I was unable to speak it.

I describe Arribeños 1499 in detail because after Japan entered World War II we stayed at home a lot and came to know the house and gardens to the fullest. Every nook and cranny became a dear friend.

Michael Ham

I'm getting quite good at knotting ties, I thought as I looked at myself in the mirror. I wore ties to Frances Holland School, then Elmwood School, and now to Michael Ham, with the familiar tunic and hat; however, this time they were navy blue instead of gray or green.

Father had asked the British Ambassador and his wife whether they could recommend a good school, someplace where I could keep up my English. Sir Hillary and Lady Osborne said their daughter Esther went to Michael Ham, so I became a student there a week after arriving in Buenos Aires. As I spoke no Spanish and was used to the English school system, this seemed the ideal way to break me in gradually, with Spanish tutoring at home on weekends.

My favorite things about school were the extensive grounds and the games we played there, which I had missed in Keimei Gakuin. Michael Ham, in the beautiful suburb of Vicente Lopez, had vast grounds, in keeping with the neighborhood estates; it was an Elmwood School on a larger scale, surrounded by rolling grounds. However, the appearance was different: the trees were fewer and more tropical, including eucalyptus and palm. There were lots and lots of sweet-smelling shrubs and vines like jasmine and wisteria. Endless sunshine beat down as summer approached. It was difficult to imagine what Christmas would be like in the Southern hemisphere. I'd sit on the spotty grass, pleasantly tired and happy after a game of rounders and watch an ongoing game of field hockey. I toyed with jasmine blossoms and soaked in the sunshine.

Indoors, things were not so idyllic. Not only did everyone speak Spanish as well as English (most girls were more fluent in Spanish) but I was a Japanese entering in midterm and was an outsider many times over. Nuns ran the school, women dressed in fearfully long black robes, like witches. Some classes were in Spanish; others were in English. I was mostly in the English classes, where my classmates marveled at my British-Canadian accent. Our class mistress was very strict.

"Dolores, this is the third time I've had to tell you to stop talking."

"But Mother Spencer," Dolores replied, looking very innocent, "I wasn't talking."

"That's not true. I saw you. You are not to fib. Come here!" Dolores turned around to me, rolled her eyes, and grimaced. I giggled.

"It is not funny to tell a lie. Ayako, you come up, too."

Dolores sauntered up. Puzzled, I followed amidst whispers.

"Put out one hand, Dolores." Dolores hid her hands behind her back. "I said, put out your hand." Dolores put out her left hand. Mother Spencer took a ruler from her desk and lifted it above her head. *Whack*! Dolores bit her lips and went back to her seat in tears.

I glared at Mother. "You have no right!"

"Silence! Put out your hand, Ayako." I hesitated, then put out my left hand. Mother Spencer lifted the ruler to her shoulder. *whack*. It was a much smaller whack than Dolores's and didn't hurt much, but the shock was great. I tried to smile as I walked back to my seat.

"It didn't hurt much," I whispered to Dolores.

Father was surprised. "I didn't think nuns used corporal punishment. Aren't they supposed to be sweet, unworldly things?"

"Maybe I should have a word with Mother Superior."

"Oh Mama, please don't; then everybody'll know I tattled."

"Yes, better leave it alone, Hide, unless this sort of thing continues."

A different incident wasn't left alone, though. I liked English composition class best. I was a star pupil and was glad to have one subject in which I could shine, though some of the themes stumped me, such as, "What I want to be when I grow up." Life would continue the same, wouldn't it, and when I grew up I'd be a lady like mother. Raquel wrote that she wanted to be a ballerina, Amelia wanted to be a doctor, and Dolores wanted to marry a handsome millionaire and live in a big house. I had never thought that one's life could change in the future, and I was shocked at Dolores for talking about money. Even thinking of filthy lucre was the height of vulgarity.

This "different incident" occurred during composition class. Mother Spencer announced, "We're going to have ten of you who speak good English appear in a play on a special night for parents." Ten meant half the class. "Raquel, Amelia, Monica Cardona, Carolyn, Evangelina (a groan—she hated appearing in plays), Marcela, Monica Saenz, Fiona, Lucia…how many do we have?…nine…" Me, I thought. I can speak better than any of them. Let it be me. "How about Carmen, and in case someone gets sick, Elena, can you be understudy? Quiet, girls, quiet." In the excited babbling, I sat silent. Why had I not been called? I loved to act in plays.

At home, mother ferreted out the reason I was so dejected and had a word with Mother Spencer.

"This is for a 'Wings for Churchill' evening and we thought you might not wish your daughter to take part in it."

"We'd be pleased to have our daughter appear in any event the school sponsors if she meets the standard."

Mother Spencer was quite short with me. "I hear you want to appear in the play. Here's a part we added for you at the end."

Father and mother were in the auditorium as I appeared on stage. Some people had already started to get up as I declaimed, "I am the eternal flame…"

After more plays and songs by older students, refreshments were served.

"Evangelina, you were excellent." "Carolyn, you were wonderful." I walked towards my parents as a mustached British colonel lifted his eyebrows and commented, "She looks Japanese to me," not bothering to lower his voice.

Esther Osborne, a senior surrounded by people, smiled and came over. "You sounded just like an English girl, and your dress *is* pretty!"

Sir Hillary, the British ambassador, and Lady Osborne came over and shook hands with father and mother.

"How good of you to come on the Wings for Churchill evening—and your daughter was excellent," Sir Hillary beamed.

"Charming," said Lady Osborne. "I think your daughter was one of the best." I felt less yellow and ugly.

"We spent so many happy years in England that of course we wanted to be here tonight," father replied, and the four chatted pleasantly till people started looking. The man with the mustache stared curiously, then came over to be introduced.

Between Sra. Gomez, who tutored me at home, and the girls at school, I began picking up Spanish. Eventually, I began inviting classmates to my home.

"Come for tea on Saturday and let's play before we eat the goodies." The garden was perfect for hide and seek (the grotto, the gazebos, the shrubs around the gardener's house—although that might have to be out of bounds) and big enough for a challenging game of tag.

"I'd love to come," answered Mónica Cardona, Amelia, Raquel, Evangelina, Dolores, and Lucia. I didn't really want to invite Lucía, but since I'd invited Evangelina…

"Come at two o'clock then."

"Two o'clock! I'll still be having lunch!"

I remembered Marie in Ottawa. "Oh come on, let's have lots of time to play."

"Well…"

"Two-thirty then."

"All right, I suppose…"

Saturday was a beautiful day, just right to play outdoors. Two-thirty came, but nobody arrived. Three o'clock. I heaved myself up on the horizontal bar in the playground as I waited. Three thirty. Maybe they think it's next Saturday. I think I'll call Raquel's house. "Raquel! You're still there! Aren't you coming today?"

"I'm just about to leave. I'll be there in half an hour."

"Half and hour! But I said two thirty. Nobody's here yet."

"It's only three thirty. Everyone'll start coming around three thirty or four." And so it was, with elaborate excuses, all except Lucía, who'd probably forgotten.

"I'm terribly sorry to be late, Ayako, but my cousin dropped in and I just couldn't get away."

"I was all ready to leave, then I had one phone call after another."

The girls wore party frocks with ribbons and lace trimmings, hardly the thing for tag and hide and seek, which we played anyway. Tea was served at five, an hour and a half late. Everyone was perspiring, hair disheveled, ribbons undone, some lace torn. The girls seemed happy to come in; nobody asked to play outside longer and there was much "oohing" and "aahing" over the sumptuous tea our cook had prepared.

Lucía arrived. "Am I late? I'm awfully sorry. I left quite early, but we lost our way and then we had engine trouble."

"It's almost time to be fetched."

"Oh no, my father won't fetch me till nine."

"Nine!" My parties had ended around five, at the latest, six.

Raquel was fetched at seven, and the others left around eight, except for Lucía, whose father came at nine. They poked around the rooms and admired the house and furniture, they talked and giggled about boys, we played some Monopoly, and it became frightfully boring. When did they have dinner? At seven thirty we all had dinner with my parents, because it was our dinner time. They seemed to enjoy meeting Father and Mother ("So handsome!" "So beautiful and elegant." "So nice!") but didn't have much appetite after that late, heavy tea.

Mother asked my tutor, Sra. Gomez, about children's parties. Sra. Gomez laughed.

"Sra. Baronesa, girls' parties usually start at four or five and last till around nine."

"Why didn't they say they couldn't come at two thirty?"

"They were being polite. Better just to come late. It's considered bad form to come on time anyway."

"I thought it was rude to be late!"

"Not at all, and this is even truer for adult gatherings. Except for official functions, the more important you are, the later you come."

"I guess I didn't notice the custom, since we mostly go to diplomatic gatherings where everyone's on time."

"Of course, you must offer elaborate excuses—that's part of the show: how you received a phone call just as you were going out, how you forgot your purse and had to turn around…"

"I'm very bad at making excuses. What shall I do? And dinner? What time do the children dine?"

"Well their main meal is at lunchtime and they usually have a light dinner around nine. A nice high tea is always welcome, so yours must have been much appreciated."

Sure enough, Mónica Cardona's party started at five and the small, dark house overflowed with friends, relatives, and grownups, too. We played games and ate a lot. I was reminded of Marie's parties in Ottawa. Evangelina O'Farrell's party was at four and our friends from school played on the swings and with the dog and cat. I enjoyed myself thoroughly. At Lucía's, there were girls from school and cousins, several of them boys. I was conscious that there were boys because of the giggling that went on ("Raul is cute!"). The boys were arrogant and ignored us.

By November 1941, I was happy at Michael Ham. I spoke Spanish passably well now and had been put in a more advanced class, but I still kept my friends from Miss Spencer's days, especially Raquel, whose home I visited often and who often visited mine. Raquel, who spoke fluent English, was the only daughter of an industrialist who had emigrated from Germany years before. She was polished and poised but versatile enough to join in any manner of play, however childish or strenuous, and she included me in her circle of friends from school, a sophisticated Spanish-speaking group. For my part, I listened and smiled a lot. Our fathers also knew each other well. Most of the "Anglo-Saxon" group with which I shared a lot in common were not friendly to me, though Evangelina was an exception, and some of the girls who actively sought me out at school let slip comments like, "How lovely to have an ambassador for a father," "You must live in a very large house," "I wish I were rich like you," which surprised, then disconcerted me. I would have to be on my guard. With Dolores, who had taken me under her sloppy wing, I could relax, and she was always funny and kind, but I was too earnest to really relate to her lighthearted ways. In Raquel I found friendship and safety.

Learning Spanish and Making Friends with the Downstairs

"We must all learn Spanish, *aprendamos español*," Father had said soon after Mother and I arrived in Buenos Aires, "although everyone seems such a good linguist here that I can get along in English or German."

"I'll need Spanish to speak to the servants. And Masako's the one who will need it most, even if she does go to Michael Ham."

"Right. A Berlitz teacher's been coming every morning, and I've made some progress—no trouble with *Buenos días, cómo está,* and that sort of thing—but at our age, sorry, I should speak for myself, I don't learn that fast."

"'Our age' is right. You're very good at languages, but I'm not. I get them all mixed up."

"Ayako will learn in no time. Spanish is much easier than English or French or German."

Mother took lessons after Father each morning from his Berlitz teacher, Sr. Sanchez, often complaining about how difficult the sessions were. I was taught not by a Berlitz expert, but by a widow in her late twenties, Sra. Gomez, who came on Saturdays, Sundays, and Wednesdays, when school was half-day.

"*Buenos días. Cómo le va hoy?*" The familiar *tu* was still too difficult for me. Sra. Gomez had creamy skin, violet eyes, and black hair that she pulled back into a bun, which did nothing to hide her beauty.

"*Muy bien gracias y usted?*" Locky was curled up at my feet, also learning Spanish. Buenos, a fox terrier who joined our family soon after we arrived, was too frisky for our sessions, and besides, he didn't need any Spanish lessons. Sra. Gomez wore black at first, then gray, and she had a silver cross in each pierced ear. I was eager to please, and after a month of lessons and going to school, I spoke well enough to carry on a more interesting conversation, something not out of our textbook. Sra. Gomez had now started wearing lavender, though all her dresses were still simple. She looked especially pretty in lavender, a lighter hue of her violet eyes.

"*Porqué no usa negro o gris ahora?*" Why do you no longer wear black or gray?

"*Ya es más de un año desde que falleció mi marido.*" It's more than a year already since my husband passed away.

"*Qué es falleció?* What is 'to pass away?'

"*Morir.*"

"?"

"To die," she said with a heavy accent that made her voice guttural.

"*Ah. Cómo era el Sr. Gomez?*" What was he like?

Sr. Gomez had been an older man and a tyrant. Why had she married him? She had been very young; her parents were for the match and she had been swept off her feet. She was sorry he had suffered a heart attack but was secretly relieved to be free of him.

Two months and I was fluent, though my vocabulary could have been larger.

"*Pero habla perfectamente.*" Ayako speaks perfectly! Sra. Gomez was very proud, and mother switched her lessons from Sr. Sanchez to Sra. Gomez.

"Sr. Sanchez makes it very difficult, and he so condescending when I can't follow."

Father smiled and said nothing. Father was doing very well with Sr. Sanchez.

One Wednesday I asked Sra. Gomez, "*Porqué no se casa otra vez?*" Why don't you marry again? Sra. Gomez confided that there was a certain Sr. Palou who had liked her even before she married and whom she had grown to like, too. They might marry now that the period of mourning was over. Lucky man, I thought. Sra. Gomez made everything she touched dainty and beautiful. Her clothes were simple but on her they were as elegant as Mother's. She drew flowers on the covers of her ordinary notebooks and they became dainty, too. "Will you invite me to the wedding?"

"I'd like to, if we do decide to marry, but only our families would be coming, because it's a second wedding for me." Seeing my disappointment, she added, "Perhaps your mother would let you come for tea sometime later and you could meet Antonio."

"Oh, I'd *love* to see your place, but doesn't Sr. Palou work?"

"He works in a store, not far. They have a long lunch break, so he can join us for a little while if you come around 3:00, maybe on a Wednesday, and we can have a lesson before tea."

The wedding must have already been planned, for by mid-November Sra. Gomez, now Sra. Palou, had returned from a short honeymoon and settled down. Sr. Palou had moved from his bachelor's quarters to her apartment. She remembered her promise and asked mother whether I could come for a lesson and tea.

"*Mucho amable, invita usted mía hija,*" Much nice you invite mine daughter. Mother could communicate now, but she couldn't be bothered with grammar. Father, with Sr. Sanchez and his Berlitz, spoke more slowly but correctly. "You should change to Sra. Palou—her classes are much more interesting than Sr. Sanchez's."

"I'll stay with the present arrangement. The trouble is I really don't have much chance to use my Spanish; everyone's such a linguist here. Besides, it wouldn't do to speak broken *castellano* like some people."

"Pride, pride."

Besides my textbooks, I took Yardley's lavender cologne, which I knew Sra. Palou liked, plus flowers and a silver bonbon dish from mother. The apartment was on a busy street with an electrical appliance store on the ground floor. *Bzzzzzzzz.* I had thought Sra. Palou's doorbell would tinkle.

"*Bienvenida! Entre por favor!*" Welcome! Please come in!

It was the first time I had been in an apartment since coming to Buenos Aires. There was a living-dining room, a small, neat kitchen, and in the back, I was told, a bedroom, from where Antonio would emerge in a minute. Trucks hurtled below the windows and there was a gray building in front. The sofa and chairs were dark brown, the rug was a dark brown pattern, and two windows facing the street let in much-needed light. I had expected Sra. Palou to be surrounded by blue and lavender silk. ("Dark colors are more practical; besides, there were Sr. Gomez and now Sr. Palou's tastes to consider," Mother said afterwards.) The cushions, at least, were soft beige silk. Sra. Palou fluffed one up on the sofa besides her. "Come and sit down and tell me what you have been doing in school."

Sr. Palou walked in. He was of medium build, ordinary, and brown like the furniture: brown hair, a brown suit, and wrinkled brown skin. He was old, already forty by my estimation. I was shocked that this was the man who had loved Sra. Palou for years and years and whom she had chosen to marry.

"*Mucho gusto, Srta. He oído tanto de usted.*" Pleased to meet you, miss. I've heard so much about you. He glanced at Sra. Palou, who smiled a special smile and looked very happy. I felt indignant and let down. How could she marry such a battered, ordinary man and look so radiant? He sat down and talked to me for a few minutes. Then he stood up to return to work and kissed my teacher on the way out. ("A widow becomes lonely and has a hard time in the world," said Mother later, "and looks and youth are not that important in a marriage.")

The afternoon passed pleasantly, Sra. Palou proving to be a charming hostess, but the expectation, the glow, was gone.

A month after arriving in Buenos Aires, my Spanish had become good enough to satisfy my curiosity about life downstairs, usually the first thing I set to find out, as I had made good friends with the staff in San Francisco and Ottawa: Ikeda, Kate, and Jack.

The basement dining room, next to the kitchen, was large, the first room you entered as you descended from the back entrance (Takada the cook fiercely defended the huge kitchen itself from my entry). The table, which could seat fourteen, made the dining area a jolly stopping place for tradesmen, errand boys, and relatives. They exchanged laughter and gossip over coffee, which was served by whomever on the staff was free. Even Takada occasionally joined in, though he couldn't understand the rapid talk. If I poked my head in, a chair would be pulled out for me, the talk became decibels quieter, and then half those present said thanks for the coffee and suddenly remembered they had to continue their work. This semi-basement was half above the ground, with all the rooms having windows which alleviated the darkness.

"Zulema, can I see your room?" Zulema, who used no makeup on her fine features, not even lipstick, was my maid and good friend, as well as being a general maid. "Refined," Mother had said, "though she has a mind of her own."

"There's not much to look at, but come in."

It was true. There was a bed and a bedside table with a clock, a dresser with hairbrush and comb, a stiff-backed chair, a table and chair, and a wardrobe. It was a very neat and bare room. No flowers, perfume, or books. I studied the lone photograph on the table, of Zulema's parents, sister (a Zulema with makeup and flashy clothes), and Zulema herself. I looked at the frosted-glass lampshade on the ceiling light and had an idea.

"Let's change the lampshade. I saw lots of them in a room in the basement left over from before." I found a colorful shade and showed it to mother before handing it to Zulema. "Mama, look what I found among the junk in the basement."

"Imitation Tiffany glass, a lampshade to brighten up any room, though Zulema may prefer something simpler." Mother looked interested.

"Isn't it too colorful?" was indeed Zulema's reaction, but at my insistence she hung it anyway.

"Can I see your room?" I asked Maria the housekeeper. She and her husband, Isamu Takeoka, our chauffeur, looked alike: fiftyish, with leathery skin and bucked teeth generously displayed during their frequent laughter, though Maria was short and plump and Takeoka tall and lean. Maria's parents had emigrated from Kyushu and ran a small laundry, like many Japanese. Buenos-Aires-born Maria, who spoke only Spanish, had been instilled with the spirit of hard work, loyalty, and an honesty that made some of her friends laugh. The only outward sign of this inner discipline in her motherly appearance was her straight black hair, pulled back into a bun at the nape of her neck. Her husband, Isamu, Okinawan born, still understood Japanese but couldn't speak it after years of using only Spanish at home and work. He was an easy-going man who looked like Disney's Goofy, but he shared Maria's upstanding principles, so that the two formed the backbone of the downstairs.

Maria threw up her hands. "You can see our rooms, but they're a mess." The two large, dark rooms were a mess. Not that they were untidy or dirty; it was just that they were crammed with a huge bed, dresser, wardrobes, tables, chairs, bureaus, and knickknacks: photographs, plastic flowers, china dolls, calendars, magazines, cigarettes, ashtrays, candy…there was hardly space to move. "Takeoka smokes too much," said Maria as she emptied an ashtray.

"Can I see your room, Roberto?" I asked the butler.

He smiled. "Young ladies do not look into servants' rooms." With that, he continued to polish the silver in his black and yellow striped waistcoat, his morning uniform. He was always correct and efficient, kept his own counsel, and was smart in whatever he did. Father had said once to Mother, "Roberto has perfect training and knows all about wines—often guests' favorite wines, too. In fact, he knows so much about the guests, he sometimes makes me wonder." An under-butler came to help him later, Otto Mueller, a handsome rosy-cheeked country boy whom Roberto trained just enough to help him (but not enough to compete with him) and who left after two years to join the army. Roberto was replaced soon after Japan entered World War II by a nice Austrian whose delicate health led to his being replaced in turn by a Japanese Jack-of-all-trades. By far, Roberto was the most skilled, if not the most trustworthy, of the butlers. By the time I knew enough not to pry into the lifestyles of the downstairs, he had left.

"Zulema, why doesn't Roberto let me see his room? I even saw him locking his door, as if anybody would go in without asking."

"Maybe he doesn't want little girls like you to be snooping around."

"Maybe he's hiding a corpse." But if anyone was hiding a corpse, it was more likely to be Takada, who drank and beat his wife, or Jorge and Elena, the furtive couple-of-all-work who came three times a week until they left one day, never to return.

"So, it's corpses you're looking for. It's a good thing you're away at school most of the week, although you'd think they'd teach you more sense at a fancy British school."

Japan Enters World War II

It was a December morning in 1941. As I lingered in bed waiting for Zulema to wake me up, I heard voices: Father's, Mother's, and other men's voices. Strange, I thought, that there should be guests at this hour. There were sounds of doors opening and closing, a general rushing around. I sat up. Zulema should have shaken me with *Hora de levantarte,* time to get up, long ago. I padded out to the hallway. Mother was just coming up the stairs, fully dressed and looking tired.

"What's the matter, Mama?"

"Get back into bed, dear. You're not going to school today. Something terrible has happened and I've been up all night."

I was now wide awake. "Is Papa sick?"

"No, nothing like that. I shouldn't have blurted it out like that, but I couldn't help myself. So I might as well tell you straight away: Japan and the United States are at war! I can't tell you more now, because I came upstairs to look for something for your father and I'm in a hurry." With that, Mother disappeared into her bedroom.

I was relieved that nothing had happened to Father but knew that war was something serious and dreadful, people killing other people. I crawled back into bed and tried to think about war. England and Germany were at war. Japan had been fighting in China, and Fiona and Heather at Frances Holland had not played with me because of that. I thought of 192 Daly Avenue and Jack the chauffeur's eldest son, who had been so proud to be in uniform. I thought of my cousin Makoto, who wanted to become a soldier like his father, chivalrous Makoto. I thought of the soldier, his face disfigured with anger as he shouted "*bakayaro!*" (Idiots!) on the tram. *Hijohji, hijohji*—war was very *hijohji*. I thought of the mustached man at the Wings for Churchill concert and the Anglo-Saxon girls at Michael Ham who kept away from me. Still, the pictures of soldiers in trenches, planes dropping bombs, and tanks crumbling buildings seemed remote. I got up and changed by myself, as Zulema seemed not to be coming this morning, and rang for breakfast.

"*Japón ha declarado guerra. Vuelven todos?*" Japan's declared war. Are you all going back? Zulema was very excited as she brought an orange, a soft-boiled egg and toast, and Ovaltine into the breakfast room.

In the evening, I was able to catch Father at last for a few minutes. "Papa, why are Japan and America fighting? Are we all going back?"

Father looked old. "We're fighting because the Japanese military are stupid; they can never win a war against America! No, no, forget that I said that. I didn't really mean it. Japan and America are fighting because Japan needs to buy and sell freely and needs more land, too—it's such a small country with so many people. President Roosevelt of the United States kept pushing Japan into a corner until it could stand it no longer."

"Oh. Is Japan going to win the war?"

"I hope so. The Japanese are very brave, but America has such vast resources. It's difficult to tell yet. And as for going back, Argentina's a friendly, neutral country, so we'll stay here—you won't have to leave your friends. My job is to see that Argentina remains neutral. Little Japan already has enough enemies."

"Then why aren't I going to school today?"

"Your friends will be talking about the war, and Mama and I thought it would be easier for you to stay at home today."

I never did not go back to Michael Ham, Mother explaining that "the Christmas holidays will be starting soon and we may change your school after the long summer vacation."

"Why?"

"A Spanish school might be less awkward."

Were my friends not to be friends anymore? I wanted to go to Raquel's but knew that this was not the time. War meant people died. I thought of the pictures in the papers that Father and Mother so avidly read, of houses destroyed by German and English bombs, of children covered in blood and crying. Would Masa be fighting? Would he be killed? Changing schools was a very small thing. I was quiet and on my best behavior for the next few weeks, spending a lot of time with Locky and Buenos in the garden.

Many people came to the house, and Father and Mother were up till late every night with embassy staff. Christmas came and went quietly. It wasn't like the Christmases I had known, being hot and midsummer in the Southern Hemisphere. Most of my friends had gone to the resorts of Mar del Plata, Nahuel Huapi or Punta del Este. With Japan at war, Papa said we would "keep a low profile" in our private lives and live as simply as possible. He did not pass up official functions however, as they seemed important in Argentina to maintain the image of a powerful and confident nation.

During lunch one day, Mother said to Father, "This morning when I went to Gath & Chavez to run some errands, I found myself in the same elevator with the Osbornes, and our eyes met. As I wondered what to do, Sir Hillary said, "Good morning" without his usual smile and Lady Osborne nodded wordlessly. I mumbled, "Good morning" and we rode in silence till the third floor, where I got off. It seemed like a very long ride."

"Yes, it's sad. Sir Hillary and I take great pains to avoid each other at official functions. I talk a lot with von Staegel and Braun now; the trouble is Braun has such bad breath and smells of rotten sausages."

"Really! He's probably saying nasty things about you, too."

"I was just being facetious to cheer you up. Japan is fighting for its life, and of course the more goodwill we can create here, the better."

"Yes. My heart aches when I think how much Masa, your mother, our families and friends—everyone in Japan—must be suffering while we live in this land of plenty." Mother had tears in her eyes.

Life Resumes

We did not go anywhere during the hot summer, and Sra. Palou came every weekday except when she went away with Sr. Palou for two weeks to Mar del Ajo. In my child's world, war seemed far, far away. Mother continued her lessons twice a week and I took additional private lessons to catch up on history, geography, and other subjects that Argentine girls my age all studied.

The dogs always kept me company. When we had first come to Arribeños, Mother, seeing the size of the garden, decided that Locky could do with a friend. She chose a wire-haired fox terrier for his cheerfulness.

"We'll call him Buenos Aires!"

"But Mama, that's much too long. How about Juan or Pedro?"

"Uninteresting. Besides, we can call him Buenos."

And Buenos he was called. Locky took the pup in hand and taught him to stalk and kill cats, for Locky wanted revenge.

When we first arrived, Locky had sniffed at a large tomcat in neighborly fashion, thinking he was a friend.

"Meow! Phhhz-phhhz!" a paw lashed out and scratched Locky's right eye.

"Yap! Yap! Owwwwoooo!" Locky howled with surprise and pain. The tomcat sauntered away.

Locky was not blinded; he fully recovered and his dormant terrier hunting instincts were revived, with a black hatred towards all cats. He was kept busy because every noon two spinsters left food for the strays at the corner of Loreto and Luis Maria Campos. The cats feasted, then jumped into our garden for a little siesta. They were soon disturbed by a short-legged white dog that came charging madly with a frisky fox terrier pup in tow. Although the cats usually managed to escape up one of the plentiful trees, a peaceful siesta was no longer possible with the "bow-wow-wows" underneath.

Very occasionally, a cat panicked and froze, and strong Westie jaws clamped down on its throat. Locky had become smart and there were no more scratched eyes. There were never any dead cats in the garden, either.

"What a thoughtful gardener Juan is," Mama said, thankful. "Even with an assistant, he has more than enough to do, but he always manages to remove dead cats so fast."

I mentioned this to Zulema and Maria when we were chatting about Locky's rounds.

"Ha!" snorted Maria, "Juan does that because the Barretos next door hate cats and offer one peso for each dead cat in the neighborhood. Juan even sets traps."

"I don't believe you"

"Look under the hedge between the Barretos' garden and ours, especially near Juan's house at the bottom—and don't touch anything if you want to keep your fingers."

I went searching, first around the top near the jasmine, then under the hedge. Nothing. A little further down, the watchdog *teru-teru* birds scurried past. They did not scream "teru-teru," because they knew me now. Under the hedge lay an ugly metal trap, like the bear traps I had seen in books. Next, past the fig trees and bushes that hid the garden near Juan's house, the garden area filled with greenhouses, seedlings, empty pots, and a vegetable patch. No traps here. Under the hedge near a fig tree? Yes, here was another trap. Something tan and furry was writhing in it. Shocked, I ran back to the house. "Mama, there's a cat dying in one of Juan's traps!"

Mother forbade Juan to set any more traps, not going into more detail than "the dogs may get caught in them," but Maria said he continued anyway. I never checked again.

The cats faced additional danger as Buenos grew and became a skilled hunter under Locky's tutelage. Locky had been a nuisance, but the longer-legged and younger Buenos was a formidable enemy for any cat foolish enough to jump into our garden.

Buenos had a special bark when he cornered a cat: "Wa-aarf!"

Locky dropped whatever he was doing and dashed off towards the "Wa-aarf!" as fast as his short legs would permit. Once, when I lay in the hammock under the pine tree, I saw the dogs' ritual. Hearing the "Wa-aarf!"I twisted myself into an *X*, toes pointed upwards, face down, and watched with horrible fascination. Buenos was waving his tail but snarling fiercely on top of a tabby, jabbing and keeping it down, waiting for Locky to come. Locky rushed in and delivered the coup de grace, sinking his teeth into the jugular. The two dogs sniffed the dead cat, then Buenos rolled over on his back, fawning at Locky, who bristled with excitement and wagged his tail in approval. Buenos did not hate cats, but he enjoyed the hunt and wanted to please his mentor.

My parents were unable to curb Locky and Buenos once they smelled their prey, so Mother asked the two spinsters whether they could feed the cats elsewhere—it would certainly be kinder and prolong their lifespan. The ladies agreed with bad grace; they had been feeding cats at that corner for thirty years and felt that the garden was ideal for a siesta—couldn't we just tie up the dogs? Afterwards the killings decreased dramatically, though they did not entirely stop, as cats still wandered in and the dogs knew the favored routes.

Buenos really preferred caddying for Father, who loved golf but thought it frivolous to play when Japan was at war. His score was around seventy, Mother's in the high nineties. Father began practicing with his nine iron from the bottom of the garden, and Buenos sat ten feet in front, from where he would run uphill towards the house and retrieve; it was uncanny how he'd sniff out that particular ball, ignoring all others that might be lying in the vicinity.

"Let me try," Mother said one day. Buenos cocked his head and moved to the side, level with Mother. *Clink.* The ball bounced low uphill with Buenos in hot pursuit. "How did he know he might be hit if he stayed in front?" Mother said, laughing.

"Better than a caddy."

The summer holidays were over and it was time to go to school again. I was taken to see the Sacred Heart, where a gorgeous purple wisteria climbed up to the second floor in the inner courtyard. However, French as a second language was a must and my parents wanted me to keep up my English. It was decided that I would transfer to a Spanish convent only seven blocks from home.

Father was pleased. "It's walking distance, much more convenient than Michael Ham or even the Sacred Heart. You can choose English as a second language, too, and the nuns seemed very friendly and sweet and eager to help you fit in."

"But Papa, what a horrible name: *Colegio de las Esclavas del Sagrado Corazón de Jesus! Esclavas* means 'slaves.' Are we all going to be slaves?!"

"No, no, in English the school is translated as 'The Handmaidens of the Sacred Heart,' and it's the nuns who are the handmaidens."

A week after I changed schools, Raquel, who had been in Mar del Plata, invited me for lunch, just the two of us.

"The Staegers came originally from Germany—it was nice of them to invite you," said Father.

"Does that matter? Raquel is my friend."

"I know and there are probably many other friends who'd like to invite you and who'd like to come over and play. But you're not just another Japanese girl; you're the Japanese ambassador's daughter, and that makes some parents hesitate. They don't want to be seen as pro-Japanese."

"Are there many Argentineans of German descent?" Mother steered the conversation away from its current course.

"There are more of Spanish and Italian descent, of course, but the German and British communities have powerful business interests. Despite the Falkland Islands issue and expressions like *ir a la inglesa,* which literally translates as 'going English' but means 'going Dutch' (!), the low-profile English are better liked than the heavy-handed Germans and Americans right now."

"How about those of Japanese descent?"

"Unlike in Brazil, there are so few of them, they hardly make a dent. But there are even fewer Chinese, so at least they're not mistaken for Chinese as they are in the other countries we've been to."

"At Michael Ham, Lucia asked me whether you were a laundryman."

Father laughed. "Instead of the Chinese laundryman you have the Japanese laundryman—many of them, too. The very successful settlers grow flowers on a large scale, like the Tomodas. But you notice their children go to university, so we'll be seeing a change in professions in the next generation. Also there's no racial prejudice here; you're accepted as an Argentinean if you speak the language well."

"Mónica Cardona first thought I was Argentinean because I had an Argentine accent."

"See? Where else except in Latin America would a Japanese be taken for granted as a native? Where you're automatically naturalized after five years unless you don't want to be? Well, anyway, to get back to what we were talking about, you're going to Raquel's, Ayako?"

"Yes, this Saturday for lunch."

"Give my best regards to Sr. Staeger."

We had lunch by ourselves near a bay window on the second floor overlooking the vast garden. We talked about Michael Ham, the Esclavas, Mar del Plata, and Locky and Buenos.

Sr. and Sra. Staeger came in, both tall, blonde and smiling, as we were finishing dessert. "I hope you are having a good time."

"Oh yes, thank you."

"How is your father?"

"He's very well, thank you, and he sends you his best regards."

"Wars, wars, dreadful things. Germany's been at war for a long time. Argentina is the best place in the world to be right now."

We played in the garden, but I was less carefree than before. Raquel was the same, the friendly and poised Raquel I knew, but somehow I felt watched (by whom?). We vowed to be friends always.

"Come to my house again."

"Yes, and come to mine. *Hasta Pronto*. Until soon."

As the war progressed there was cautious joy at home. It was going better than Father had dared to hope.

"We've taken the Solomon Islands and the Gilbert Islands, on top of Singapore, Burma, and the Philippines. What fighting spirit can do! But now comes the hardest part, holding on to these places."

The joy was short lived.

Colegio de las Esclavas del Sagrado Corazón de Jesus

The nuns wore long habits as in Michael Ham, and I was still knotting ties (navy blue with red stripes this time), but there were many more hours of religion. The catechism started with, "Why am I a Catholic? I am a Catholic by the Grace of God."

I was not a Catholic—I had no religion—so how should I answer in a way that showed I had done my homework? I said, "I am not a Catholic by the Grace of God," and Mother Esperanza was scandalized.

There was a lot of memorization and maps to trace, and good conduct was very, very important. I found that except for math class, if I behaved well, my marks remained high without much effort. My weekly report card had one column under *conducta*, mostly with full marks of 10 for good behavior, and another column under *aplicación,* with mostly 8s for effort. The combined result wasn't bad.

I learned Argentine history, some of which I had already gleaned from Sra. Palou. San Martin, the national hero, had made his epic march across the Andes in 1817 with 5,000 men. I remembered looking down from the plane at the snow-covered mountains.

To spur us on to more diligence, we were told that children in the National Schools slogged to classes even in the pouring rain, so why should a mere drizzle or so deter us from walking to school, to say nothing of those who came by car. In the schools I had attended up till now, only heavy snow or a typhoon were elements fierce enough to justify missing classes. Would heavy rain have been an excuse? I had watched the children of the National Schools with interest; they were conspicuous in their white overalls, worn over their clothes like a uniform. Once you got used to the sight, it was cheerful to see boys and girls all so immaculate. Sometimes their teachers also wore matching white coveralls.

I was one of those driven to school (the morning was always rushed), but on the way back, I walked in fair weather with Zulema, who carried my case, heavy with books. This type of leather suitcase, thicker than an attaché case, was standard fare, and I must have walked home by myself after a while, because my right shoulder is now an inch lower than my left with the weight of those books. The walk was very pleasant, past Zelmira's ultra-modern glass and concrete house, Olga's home, which was small and cozy, and Elena's old-fashioned mansion, surrounded by grounds as large as ours but darkened by overgrown trees and shrubs. Elena was very nice and very bright; she wanted to be a doctor. She was also round and short like her mother, who always wore black and went to church in an old black Rolls Royce driven by a black-liveried chauffeur. On religious holidays the whole length of their iron fence was draped in yellow and white, "the colors of the Church," according to Zulema, who was a Catholic but never attended Mass. By the time we saw the home of the Barretos, the cat-haters (Juanita was two classes above me), we knew that we were almost home.

Father had bought the first secretary's old car, a discolored navy blue Ford, and to Takeoka's dissatisfaction he had to take me to school in that plebeian car instead of the sleek official Cadillac. He found an excuse to drive me in the Cadillac when he had to take Father somewhere immediately afterwards. One such morning, after I was driven to school in the big car, my classmate Zelmira asked, "Is it the custom in Japan to bow a lot? I was watching from the window and I saw this huge Cadillac drive up. The driver got out, bowed to the back seat, opened the door, took off his cap, and bowed again. Then *you* stepped out and as you ran up the steps he bowed to you twice more. I thought at least a cardinal had come."

"Does Takeoka bow that much? I never noticed."

"Well, look the next time, Your Highness."

Sure enough, though Zelmira exaggerated, Takeoka bowed a lot. After I pointed this out to Father, the bows decreased to one.

"We don't want to be conspicuous right now, though we must maintain dignity. Appearances shouldn't be sneezed at."

There were sewing lessons and embroidery lessons, petticoats to sew and handkerchiefs to embroider, which I despised. Calligraphy class, with its swirling letters and Gothic capitals, was more fun than at Keimei, and my improving skills reflected that. I took up piano again, and this was also enjoyable, partly because not all was Czerny. We got to play Chopin, Beethoven, and Schubert as well. Partly, also, because I was taught by Mother Avelina. She was young, radiant, and flatteringly encouraging, with an innocence that shamed me.

"Why, that's very good, Ayako." "Splendid." "You are so musical." "You didn't practice? Well, I suppose you had a lot of other homework because you usually prepare so well." "You forgot your music books? I have some extra ones. Just practice while I get them."

Sports were disappointing because there was only a small concrete playground and a volleyball court. At any rate, it seemed that the girls' main concern was to move as little as possible. The rest of the grounds were taken up by the Charity School, a school taught by the nuns for free and where our older girls helped with teaching, games, and meals. The students all wore white pinafores like those at the National Schools and they often poked their heads out from the windows when we were playing. "*Hola!*" They'd wave and smile and looked very happy. Except for their white overalls, they looked and acted just like the Esclavas students, which surprised me. My image of a Charity School was influenced by *Oliver Twist,* which I had just read.

Our teachers did not lunch with us, because nuns never ate in public. Instead, the Mothers took turns reading about the life of some saint: St. Theresa of Lisieux, St. Theresa of Avila, St. Catherine of Siena. We munched in silence till dessert, when Mother marked the page with a book-marker, closed the book, and said: "*Ave Maria Purísima,*" Hail Mary, Most Pure.

We shouted, "*Sin pecado concebida!* (Conceived without sin!) and all pandemonium broke loose, for now we could talk.

Oranges were cut in half and eaten like grapefruit, which was not easy because they were so small. Grapes had to be swallowed whole because it was bad manners to spit out the skin and seeds. Mother had warned that seeds could get caught in my appendix. What to do? I didn't want to get appendicitis, but the Sisters who waited at the tables checked your plate. Looking behind at the open window, I tossed the grapes out when I thought nobody was looking. I tried not to hear Mother's words, "Don't waste food, Ayako. There are thousands of people starving in war-torn countries."

Elena, who was sitting next to me, gasped. "Hey! Did you see what Ayako did?"

"What?"

"She just tossed the grapes out the window!"

Five girls rushed to the window. "Oh, there they are, all squished!"

"Girls, what are you doing at the window? Sit down, please."

I had to write "I will not throw grapes out the window" fifty times.

Wednesdays were not half days at the Esclavas, but I could get out before the last class, which was sewing, if Mother was taking me to the opera. My parents had a box, and Mother found it a popular way to entertain wives without having to speak too much Spanish. The Teatro Colón could attract star singers like

Helen Traubel and Lorenz Melchior because the high season in Buenos Aires coincided with summertime in the Northern hemisphere. I was sometimes taken along for my musical edification and to act as translator. Verdi wasn't bad, but I hated Wagner; what I liked best were the chocolate-covered cherries and getting out of sewing class. It is because of those tiresome Wednesdays that I am now hooked on opera, the *Nibelungenlied* and all.

No classmate asked me, "Why is Japan fighting against America?" Nobody said, "I hate Japan." At school, I forgot there was a war going on, because nobody talked about it. It still seemed so far away.

It was not World War II but a revolution that really touched us in school, yet even that fear was over in a day. We were being taught history, when suddenly all classes were cancelled. Nuns and students gathered, worried and excited, and we were told to stay in our classrooms till we could be fetched because there had been a *levantamiento*, an uprising.

"A *levantamiento*! My father's in the army. I hope he's all right!" said Enriqueta.

"My father's in the government. I hope they don't shoot him!"

"Oh, I wish they'd tell us what's happening!"

"A *levantamiento*!"

"It'll be put down," said Ana Maria, whose father was Minister of Defense. She was always giggly, and her new show of calm impressed us.

I had never been in a country where soldiers shot government officials. Was this the same as war?

The military takeover affected the man on the street very little. A few shots were fired at military and government buildings, President Castillo fled to Uruguay, and the army took over power. After government returned to normal, Father and Mother gave a lavish official dinner in our big hall for the new regime.

"It was a very different group, wasn't it, from the previous government," said Father.

"They all looked alike to me in their uniforms, except for that Colonel Perón. He certainly has vitality and charm. The wives were not much different from before."

"Perón's supposed to be the up-and-coming man, the one to watch in this jousting for power. Has charisma, hasn't he."

"Do you think we should have invited Eva Duarte? Everyone knows about that actress and Perón."

"No, this is a Catholic country, and the wives would have been offended. They still refer to her as 'that two-bit conniving actress,' but if he marries her, she'll wreak her revenge!"

Kiyoko

One afternoon, the manager of a large Japanese trading firm came for tea with his wife and daughter. They had recently been transferred from New York, and Kiyoko was enrolled at las Esclavas. Perhaps we could be friends?

We hit it off immediately. Though five years younger, she was mature beyond her years, an only child who knew enough to smile "I don't know" to all questions the gossipy wife of our dentist asked about her home life. And I was still childish. Plump and always unruffled, but with a keen sense of fun and adventure, Kiyoko was game to try anything. Soon we were going back and forth to our homes, playing with our dogs (she had a fox terrier too), running in the garden, playing in the house, inventing games, dressing up and play acting, tasting the family specialties...

During our religious phase, we imitated the Catholic rites in my room.

"Let's baptize ourselves and receive Communion," I suggested.

"We're not supposed to."

"It's only make-believe."

"Then you be the priest. I want to wear the First Communion dress."

"That's not fair, Kiyoko. Why don't we take turns."

"Oh, all right."

"We need costumes and props. You be the priest first. Here, you can use my quilt for his cape. It's brocade. And I'll bring water from the bathroom in this flower vase."

"What do those getting baptized wear?"

I thought for a moment. "They're mostly babies and they wear long white things. Maybe one of Mama's nightgowns..." I couldn't find a white one, but found a light blue one.

"Pretty," said Kiyoko. "Won't she be cross if you get it wet?"

"It'll dry."

"All right, bend down. Ready?" Kiyoko emptied the vase over my head. "I baptize thee in the name of the—"

"You didn't have to use all the water! I'll use all too when *you* get baptized!"

"Don't be cross—I didn't think. Besides, I won't fit into that nightgown."

"You can wrap my sheet around you; it's white."

"How about going on to Confession and Communion. I don't mind being the priest again."

"Hmmm. If you really don't mind…here's a cushion. I can kneel on that. What can we use as a confessional?"

"Let's see…how about the folding screen in the ladies' drawing room?"

"What brains you have!"

"I'm the brainiest. I'll go and get it." Kiyoko unwrapped herself from the quilt. "It's cooler this way, too." She brought the screen, stood it in front of her, and pressed her ear to it. She only half wrapped herself in the quilt.

"I have been unkind to Buenos our dog and to Mother Esperanza. I have forgotten to say my morning and evening prayers. For these and all the other sins I may have committed, I am heartily sorry."

"For your penance, say the rosary three times, my child."

"But that's too much! Zelmira says Father Santini usually tells her to say two or three Hail Marys."

"Three Hail Marys and three Glorias then, and let's get on to Communion. Your turn to be priest. This quilt is awfully hot and I want to dress up for First Communion."

"You can use the long white veil that we use for Mass at school and my white organdy party dress."

"But I won't fit."

"Why aren't you thinner!? I know, one of the lace tablecloths for when we have guests and Mama's silver pumps."

"I suppose. And for the hosts? It's not easy, like wine."

"Coca-Cola is better than wine, and Papa's silver goblet will make a pretty chalice. The hosts…cookies? Bread? I have a wonderful idea! We'll iron some bread and flatten it!" I put on my dressing gown and ran to the basement for bread and an iron.

"What are you girls up to," asked Zulema.

"We're playing at being baptized, confessing, and receiving First Communion."

Zulema laughed. "Why don't you really become a Catholic then?"

"Don't want to. Besides, Mama says I'm too young to know yet."

We cut out little circles of bread and ironed them. We swallowed them and sipped the Coca-Cola, which spattered on the lace tablecloth.

"If you spill the wine," I said, "you really have to crawl on your hands and knees at Our Lady of Luján as penance. Old Father Arias dropped the hosts and had to do that."

When I played at Kiyoko's house, Takeoka came to fetch me at five. We had several delaying tactics, including taking a shower. The shower room had four-tiered semi-circular pipes that sprinkled water from three angles. It was fun, especially as we could climb onto the pipes and have the water tickle our bottoms.

"We're in the shower, I can't go back yet. Can't Takeoka come later?" Flushing the toilet was another ruse. "I can't come for half and hour," and the toilet would be flushed again and again.

At school, we did not see each other much, because we were in different classes. Sometimes we met at tea, which was served when we stayed till late. We drank a bitter green tea called *yerba mate*, which was similar to Japanese tea. Most girls added milk and sugar and the *mate* would turn a pea-soup color. A slice of cheese and a slice of *membrillo*, solidified quince jam, was served on a plate with bread.

I grimaced. "We're supposed to eat them together," I said as I stacked the generous slices of cheese and *membrillo* on the bread, "the cheese and this sweet stuff!"

"Delicious," said Kiyoko, who liked marmalade with bacon for breakfast.

By now I had several ethnic Japanese friends, such as sweet Amelia Kazuko, who often came to our house with Kiyoko. Carmina Yukawa and Rosamunda Shizue Konishi were almost grown ups—they had breasts and wore high heels—and I enjoyed going to discreet outings with them without my parents. It was Carmina who took me to exhibits and Rosamunda who traveled with me to Luján with her mother. Father and Mother undoubtedly felt at ease that in a time of war I was friendly with young ones whose parents were trusted friends. In addition to liking these girls, I felt able to let down my guard, which may have played a role in our spending so many happy hours together.

Kiyoko and I went to the same school again after returning to Japan, this time to the Sacred Heart. She lives in Tokyo and is one of my best friends, a sister, the only one with shared memories of early childhood.

Courtship, Japanese Style

Mother was busy in many ways, especially with the Japanese and Argentine-Japanese community.

As I began growing out of my childhood, I became delicate. The tomboy who loved tag and the horizontal bar now spent days in bed with colds. The colds were annoying but not uncomfortable enough to prevent me from reading about *David Copperfield* and *Jean Valjean*, in serious books brought by Father. I also read the romances and Screen Stories I asked Takeoka to buy for me that I much preferred. I knew all about Lana Turner's loves, Betty Grable and Harry James, and what dress Rita Hayworth wore for her wedding to Aly Khan. My colds lingered, keeping me at home for a week at a time.

"This sometimes happens to young girls as they're entering their teens," said Dr. Suzuki, who was called often by my worried mother.

"How is she today, Doctor?"

"A sore throat, Baroness, and 37.4-degree fever. Let's take care that it doesn't develop into bronchitis, as it sometimes does with your daughter. Stay a few days in bed, take a week off from school, and drink lots of liquids."

"There are so many girls with colds at school. Do you have time for tea or a drink? I'm sorry to have taken you away from your family in the evening."

"Don't worry, please. I'm a bachelor, so there's nobody waiting. Yes, I would love a drink."

"Scotch? Brandy?"

"Thank you, I could use some brandy after a hard day. Everyone seems sick. Come to think of it, though, I'm driving, so I'd better have tea." Dr. Suzuki twirled his mustache as Mother rang for refreshments. Born in Buenos Aires of 100% Japanese parentage, Dr. Suzuki looked more Latin than Oriental, but he spoke Japanese well, with only a slight accent. Slender, easy-going and appearing younger than his thirty-three years, he chatted pleasantly with Mother till he finished his tea.

One evening after I was well again, Mother said to Father during dinner, "You know, Mrs. Imai has been asking me whether I could recommend a suitable Japanese man for her eldest daughter. Mrs. Imai comes from a good Japanese family and she's taught both her daughters Japanese dance, tea ceremony, flower arrangement, and calligraphy. They're bilingual and very accomplished; the eldest has a university education, too. The Imais remain more Japanese than the others who have settled here."

"Is that so? Don't tell me you're turning matchmaker!" Father laughed. He was enjoying one of his now-rare lighter moods.

"Well, the number of eligible Japanese bachelors here is very limited. I suppose if there were no war she'd send her daughters to Japan to live with relatives to look for husbands there."

"How old is this daughter?"

"Tetsuko is twenty-nine and Mieko is twenty-seven."

"I can see the problem. But they've been born and brought up in Buenos Aires. Why shouldn't they marry Argentine men with Spanish, Italian, German, or Argentine backgrounds? It doesn't matter so much here."

"That's what I think, but Mrs. Imai and her husband won't hear of it, and it occurred to me that perhaps Dr. Suzuki…he's Argentinean and the son of a laundryman, but he's a professional man of Japanese descent, personable, and most important of all, a thoroughly nice man."

"Well, do you think he'd be interested? Maybe he already has a girlfriend, maybe several, if he's so eligible. And with all this culture and good family talk, he wouldn't want a wife who feels she's marrying beneath her."

"Dr. Suzuki is an able doctor and wonderful with patients. He has a bright career ahead of him and any girl would be lucky to get him."

"He certainly has a fan here! Who knows, a promising doctor might be just the son-in-law for the Imais."

"I think I'll talk to Mrs. Imai and Dr. Suzuki."

Mrs. Imai came for tea and Mother reported afterwards how the conversation had gone.

"I agree, Baroness, there aren't many eligible Japanese bachelors. Mrs. Fukui had kindly arranged a meeting at her house for Tetsuko with Mr. Nemoto of the Sumitomo Trading Co., but then I discovered he was a twin, and an identical twin at that."

"What's wrong with that?"

"Identical twins run in the family and I wouldn't want my poor daughter to undergo such an animal-like ordeal."

Mother had laughed. "Mrs. Imai, you're more old-fashioned than the Japanese back home! At this rate, neither daughter will get married."

A deep sigh from Mrs. Imai.

"And," continued Mother, "if I introduce Dr. Suzuki to Tetsuko-san, I must ask you to stay away at their first meeting."

"That's very unconventional."

"They can be less formal that way. I'll just introduce them and leave them alone to go out together. Tetsuko-san can invite him home for dinner at a later date if they like each other and you can look him over then. But you mustn't expect him to make a decision after one meeting in the old way."

A few days later, Mother cornered Dr. Suzuki. "I hope you won't mind my asking you a personal question, but do you have a special girlfriend?"

"Well no, but—"

"I know just the right girl for you, Dr. Suzuki."

He hemmed and hawed but agreed to a meeting at our house. I said hello to Tetsuko when she arrived. She was large-boned and masculine with thick eyebrows, and she seemed nervous and shy.

A month and a half went by and I did not catch a single cold. Mother commented on it. "I usually have to call Dr. Suzuki once every month, but you seem more used to the Argentine climate now. That's very good." She did not sound especially happy.

Right after that, I came down with a runny nose.

"Ayako, you better stay in bed because your colds always become worse. I'll call Dr. Suzuki."

"But Mama, this is nothing. Besides, it's Zelmira's birthday party tomorrow—you know I don't go to my friends' often these days."

"I know, and I'm sorry about that."

"Maybe you want me to stay in bed so that you can ask Dr. Suzuki about Tetsuko?"

Mother flushed. "I'm worried about your health."

"If I were Dr. Suzuki, I wouldn't marry Tetsuko."

"Tetsuko's a very intelligent and nice girl. Besides, how do you know all about this? You notice more than I thought. I must be careful from now on, little lady."

Dr. Suzuki came, smiling as usual. "Nothing to worry about, just a slight nose cold. Keep warm today, drink plenty of fluids, think pleasant thoughts, and you can get up tomorrow."

"Can I go to my friend's tomorrow?"

"Really, Ayako, you might get worse and miss school on Monday."

"Let's see, tomorrow is Saturday. If she's feeling all right, Baroness, I don't see why she can't go, especially as she can rest the next day."

"Well, we'll see tomorrow, so you be good today. Thank you so much for coming, Doctor. Won't you have tea or coffee?"

"Thank you, but I'm on my way to another call. Mr. Yokoi's mother. She should really be hospitalized, but she refuses to leave home."

"I'm told she's very fragile. She must be over eighty now. One of the early Japanese settlers?"

"Yes, she's so proud of her son's career as professor of mathematics at the university. By the way, Baroness, when I thanked you for introducing me to Miss Tetsuko Imai, I said I would talk to you about the development of our…er…friendship later on." He looked at me and I pretended to doze.

"Oh, don't pay attention to Ayako; she's very interested in knowing what's going to happen to her dear Dr. Suzuki."

He laughed and I opened my eyes. "Miss Tetsuko invited me to her home a couple of times. We've also gone to the cinema. She's very pleasant and I like the whole family. I especially like her sister…"

"Yes?"

"You see, Miss Tetsuko is extremely intelligent and cultured, too intelligent for a simple man like me. She's very nice, I know, but I'm afraid I'm the type who likes a sweet little woman to come home to, someone with whom I can laugh and relax. Mieko, now, has a lively sense of humor as well as being very pretty, as Miss Tetsuko is too, of course."

"But Tetsuko's the one with fine bone structure. Mieko is supposed to be quite plain, though I probably shouldn't say such a thing."

"Well, those who say that are wrong, because Mieko is feminine and lovely. I don't think she dislikes me either. Would it be very bad form if I courted Mieko instead?"

"I should think Mrs. Imai would be glad to hear you like Mieko. Of course, Mrs. Imai is terribly old-fashioned and believes the eldest should be married first, but I think I can persuade her."

"Thank you. Yes, she is old-fashioned. I was quite surprised the first evening I was invited for dinner to be told that it was a *taian,* an auspicious date. What is all this about auspicious dates?"

"In Japan, weddings and engagements take place on these *taian,* or auspicious days, and wedding gifts are given on *taian mornings.* I guess she thought it would be lucky to invite you for the first time on a *taian.* Funerals and wakes can be on *butsumetsu,* or unlucky days. You can imagine how crowded wedding reception places are on *taian* and what a bargain you could probably get on a *butsumetsu!* If your mother were still alive, she would know all about this."

"*Dios mío!* My God, I'd better begin courting Mieko on a *taian*."

Dr. Suzuki *did* marry Mieko six months later. And Tetsuko? After a year, she married a lawyer of Italian descent whom she had known at university and liked all along. Mrs. Imai was pained in the beginning about her "foreign" son-in-law, but after a while she became one of his biggest fans and was very pleased that both daughters had found happiness.

Echoes of War

In January 1944, Argentina finally severed relations with Germany and Japan, the last country on the American continent to do so. A mounted policeman now stood guard outside our gates.

At school, Zelmira whispered, "I still like you and the Japanese. I don't like Germany and America."

"Again, as in England, what's talked about at home, though your friends are fourteen years old now and not seven," said Father.

My friends would think all Japanese were like me, I thought. I had to be even more careful than before and discretion had never been my forte. "Why has Argentina 'severed relations' if people still like the Japanese? And why are they siding with the Americans if they don't like them?"

"It's very difficult to explain easily in a few sentences. You see, America has wanted Argentina to sever relations with the axis countries for a long time so that the whole American continent would stand together. And this time, with the uncovering of German spy plots here, Argentina had to sever relations or have its all-important trade with the U.S. stopped. Many Argentineans see Americans as high-handed bullies and Germans as arrogant, using Argentina just for spying. And the Japanese are seen as…well…underdogs like themselves."

"Are Japanese underdogs?"

"The Japanese are courageous and capable fighters, but the Americans have so many more resources. Nothing will break our patriotism and spirit, but we are underdogs."

"And don't Japanese spy here?"

Father smiled. "We'd be pretty conspicuous spies here, with the different color of our skin. Italians are very skilled and blend in best. People do, however, come to us with information. You'd be surprised at some of the people who come, though that's between you and me."

"I think spying is exciting."

"Spying is a dirty business, but walls have ears. There are spies everywhere; I wouldn't be surprised if my pretty, efficient German secretary were checking on us."

The embassy offices downtown were closed now. In the mornings and most afternoons Father remained in his study and the embassy staff came to Arribeños for work, converting the guest room into an office.

I continued to go to school. The mounted policeman gave a friendly salute on my way out, and I saluted back, feeling very important. The police had several shifts, and one of the basement rooms was turned over for their use, a room that had a door to the Loreto side of our garden, with its balconies. At lunchtime, when one of the shift changes took place, the gates often stood empty, while two policemen, jackets off, ate their lunch and had a smoke in their room as their horses munched grass nearby. A spring onion-like grass that grew on the verges seemed to be a delicacy. At teatime, another change of shifts occurred and two policemen would be chatting and sipping *yerba mate* in their room. Sometimes, around 1:00 P.M., five horses could be spotted in the garden with smoke rising from nearby. Five policemen sat around an *asado* barbecue drinking red wine and savoring hors d'oeuvres that Takada had made. They took turns keeping an eye on the gate.

Mother was scandalized. "Shocking," she commented

"Not at all," Father said, laughing. "We should be flattered that we need so little protection. I hear police at the German Embassy don't have such an easy time and sometimes police have to rush to the American Embassy."

"Well, that's one way of taking it. I suppose just standing there with nothing to do is dull. I'm so worried about Masa, your mother, and our families. No letters have come for six months now."

"Nor will they probably from now on. Don't expect ours to reach Japan, either; consider it a boon if they do."

Letters from Japan occasionally came through the Red Cross and the Swiss Embassy. A letter did come from Masa, though, the last one we were to receive. Uncle Yujiro had died of tuberculosis, and his widow, Aunt Ruriko, still lived with Grandmother Tomii. Makoto was in the army, and his father had been killed in China. Uncle Shiro's ship had been torpedoed and Uncle Hideo had starved in the Philippines. Uncle Takeo was somewhere in Manchuria. Grandmother Nakamura had moved to her house in Sengataki, near Kutsukake, as it was up in the mountains and safer than Tokyo. She remained amazingly strong and it was hard to persuade her to take along Aunt Akiko.

> Grandmother Tomii is very infirm now, but she refuses to move out of Tokyo. I am well and trying to study. The second engineering department of the Imperial University is in Chiba, across the bay from Tokyo, and I live in

the dorm. Sometimes, when the B29s fly over Tokyo, we watch with Ichiro's binoculars instead of going into the bomb shelters. The scene is awe-inspiring—the whole sky lights up—but we wonder whether our homes have been hit, whether our families and friends are safe. I also think of Hiro, Jiro, Yuichi, and my friends who have been drafted because they chose the liberal arts, and I wonder whether they are in any of our planes I see going down in flames.

Like all students, I work more than study. I spend a great deal of time in one of the airplane factories; I suppose I shouldn't mention which in case this is censored. We try to be as careful and efficient as possible, to help those who are defending us, but it is hard to concentrate when the main meal consists of a couple of grasshoppers in potato gruel. But it is right that those at the front have adequate rations.

You remember the two packs of cube sugar you left? I gave one box to Grandmother Tomii and Aunt Ruriko and have brought the other pack with me here to the dorm. That sugar is my treasure. It is locked in my cupboard, and when I stay at a friend's I take a cube for each member of the family and they suck in wonder, most having forgotten what sugar tastes like.

Yesterday was my birthday, so Ichiro and I had one piece each, sucking half a lump in the morning and the rest in the evening.

It is difficult for me to imagine what life in Buenos Aires is like, as so few letters come now. I hope that you are all well. I miss you all but am happy that you are in safe Buenos Aires. Ayako would surely be dead of malnutrition if she were here.

I hope this war will end soon and that we can be together again.

Mother cried. She kept all of Masa's letters in the top drawer of her bedside table and she and Father read them over and over again.

Father gave her his handkerchief. "I'm worried too. Engineering and science students are drafted last, but his turn will eventually come. I pray he won't be in one of those suicide planes or subs, though that's an unpatriotic thought. And my old mother…at least we know they are both alive and well."

"Let's write to him today."

"Now, I've told you that letters are special privileges that we should take advantage of only occasionally, though I'd like to write, too. Think of all the parents waiting for letters from the front."

"Ayako, I'm so glad you're with us."

I would never be able to put sugar in my tea again without feeling guilty. And what did grasshoppers taste like? Airplanes in flames, people killing other people…why? Father said Japan was fighting to survive because it was tiny with so many people. *Life* magazine said the Japanese were barbarians who had sneaked up on Pearl Harbor. Anger, puzzlement, and guilt raged in my soul.

The war was going badly for Japan now, and defeat after defeat followed: the Philippines, New Guineas, Saipan…Father sometimes drank alone at night and Mother was subdued.

Summer Lessons

The long summer holidays were a busy time for me. We did not go away anywhere because of the war, though it was agreed that Kiyoko and her parents
would take me with them for two weeks to a quiet beach. We spent fourteen
splendid days swimming, collecting all kinds of shells, including the large pink
conches that were in abundance, burying ourselves in the sand, building sandcas-
tles…We also collected clams by digging holes in the beach in the evening then
coming in the morning to find the holes overflowing with clams left at night by
the tide. Some people opened the clams on the beach and slurped them up on the
spot. A touch of tummy trouble only slightly marred my bliss, though it caused
Kiyoko's parents much worry.

Back at Arribeños, it was time for me to study and not waste my holidays
reading Screen Stories. My Spanish was now good enough for me to enter a class
above my present one and be with girls my age. There was no "skipping" in
Argentina, and you were tested in all subjects for the grade you wanted to skip at
school. Sra. Palou still taught Mother, but for me an efficient and impersonal
instructor came two hours every morning, five days a week. Srta. Saenz never
sparked my interest, either in herself or her subjects, but I was drilled well and
passed the exams. My schooling seemed a continual catching up, being accepted
by new classmates, then leaving.

Father was especially keen on my education. ("A girl must be able to stand on
her own two feet in this world. You can never tell what will happen.") He wanted
me to take English lessons from a native speaker during the summer holidays. It
was December 1944.

"She's forgetting her English with just the classes at school."

"But where can we find an English lady willing to teach a little enemy girl?"
Mother sounded doubtful.

"Difficult, I know, but not impossible. Just a couple of hours per week; Ayako
needs time to play too, and we don't want to burden her too much. We must
find a teacher who can awaken her interest so we won't have the disappointment
we had with her Japanese lessons."

Mr. Ukai, former head of the Japanese school, had given me lessons on Saturday mornings a year earlier, but they had been discontinued after a few months, as Father saw I was not learning much. I had not told Father that aside from Mr. Ukai not sparking my interest, I had found him cynical and resentful. My stupid mistakes moved him to mirth. "You really must study harder, because you're lucky to have a father who can afford private lessons. I'd never be able to do that for my daughter."

"My father is not rich. We try to live simply."

Mr. Ukai slapped his knees with laughter. "Well, it won't make much difference anyway. You'll marry a banker and not have to worry about anything."

He said things nobody else had dared say.

My parents were now concerned with my English.

"Oh, I agree that it's an excellent idea to keep up her English," said Mother. "The trouble is, where is this native speaker who's a good teacher too?"

Mrs. Phoebe Allen was Mother Esperanza's sister-in-law. Mother Esperanza, who had been shocked by my statement that "I am not a Catholic by the Grace of God," had ended up always looking out for me; she was a kindly, motherly nun. Mrs. Allen had come to Buenos Aires from London on an adventure, to teach English at one of the schools. She had fallen in love with Jorge Allen, an Argentinean of British descent, and never returned to England. He had died ten years earlier, and now she lived all alone in the same house she had lived in from the day she was married. Her son and daughter, both with families of their own, lived nearby. Mrs. Allen wanted to meet the young lady in question before making up her mind.

I was subdued and on my best behavior. I saw a slender old lady of about sixty with neat, short gray hair, kind blue eyes, a sharp nose, and a ramrod-straight back. What we talked about I do not remember, but at the end Mrs. Allen smiled and said, "You speak beautiful English and it would be a pity to forget it."

Three afternoons a week during the summer holidays, Mrs. Allen came in a crisp cotton dress. Mostly, we had our lessons outside on the sofa-hammock, sipping iced tea with Locky and Buenos nearby, for she loved dogs.

I wrote compositions. I also read short stories: Katherine Mansfield, Rudyard Kipling, D. H. Lawrence, and articles from magazines such as *Reader's Digest* and *Life,* as well as English-language newspapers. I preferred the everyday stuff. We talked a great deal.

"We must increase your vocabulary, including your colloquial vocabulary."

I was allowed to choose the articles and captions. "Keep your seams straight when you paint on your stockings," I read from the *Reader's Digest.*

"Shouldn't you say 'put' on your stockings, Mrs. Allen?"

"There's a shortage of stockings in America because of the difficulty in obtaining silk, so some patriotic women paint their legs, it seems. Very clever."

"At least they have food."

"Oh yes, it's a land of plenty. This is just a lighthearted caption. When you think of what's happening in Europe and Asia, this is frivolity, but sometimes frivolous things keep your spirits up. Like this ghastly caption you chose from *Life*."

"A pin-up of sweater girl Lana Turner cheers a GI," I read. "What's a sweater girl, Mrs. Allen?"

"It's one of those dreadful American expressions, used to describe a girl who fills out her sweater like this." Mrs. Allen plucked her dress at her flat breasts.

"Pretty, isn't she."

"Sexy is the correct word, but nice girls don't use that word much."

There were so many things nice girls couldn't say and do. "How do you know it then?"

"Teachers have to know a lot."

A heading from a local English paper was more acceptable: "The Equestrian Statue of Our National Hero San Martin Will Undergo Repairs."

"What's 'equestrian'?"

"It means 'on horseback' and comes from the Latin *equus*. The statue badly needed cleaning."

"You're Argentinean now, aren't you, Mrs. Allen? You married one."

Mrs. Allen put down her iced tea and pulled herself up even straighter than usual. Her starched dress crackled. "I am British and shall always be British."

"Then why are you teaching me, an enemy girl?"

"And why not? It's like asking, why do you want to keep up with an enemy language? I do what I think is right. There's too much fighting and wars; there should be a better way of settling things. You and I are friends and we're preparing the way for a better world, rather than all this killing."

"We are?"

"Yes we are. You'll see some day."

We opened the *Reader's Digest* again. I had chosen an article with the caption: "Your Reflex Action when a Burglar breaks into your Home."

"What's a 'reflex action'?"

"It's what you automatically do in response to something. For instance, if I woke up to find a burglar in my bedroom, my reflex action would be to jump out of bed, grab a lamp, and hit him over the head."

"You would? Mama says you should be quiet so as not to get hurt and let a burglar take what he wants."

"I'm not going to let any burglar just run off with things bought with my husband's hard work. Over my dead body."

I saw Mrs. Allen in a starched nightgown, gray hair in curlers, bashing a young burglar with a china lamp. I looked at her with new respect.

Mrs. Allen was not annoyed when I missed a class because of a cold.

"These aren't the easiest times, even for a young girl."

"You're never ill, Mrs. Allen, though you're old."

"True, thanks be to God." She crossed herself. "There'll be time enough when I really become old. Shall I tell you the secret of my health?"

"Some special medicine?"

"No, no, I don't believe in medicines. Every morning, even in winter, I take a cold bath."

"That's the way to catch cold!"

"No. A cold bath improves your circulation and makes you tingle all over. I haven't caught a cold in five years, touch wood." She rapped on the table, and finding it of metal, got up and knocked on a nearby grapefruit tree.

Although Mrs. Allen was old, I enjoyed our lessons and continued to see her once a week even after the new term started, though soon after I entered my new class I had to leave school again, just as I had caught up. As Mrs. Allen had said, she and I had become friends.

Internment

Argentina finally declared war against the axis countries in March 1945, and shortly after, the Spruille Braden mission came from America to make sure its ally was behaving. It was only after the mission's date was set that all Japanese Embassy-connected aliens were hastily interned.

From Arribeños came Takada the cook, who no longer chased his wife Nobu around the garden, brandishing a knife. Quiet Nobu came too. Also Adachi, who had recently been hired to butler and clean. He was an immigrant of about fifty who had retained his Japanese citizenship and whose laundry business had recently failed. His wife had left him for a smarter man; Maria said she could see why. Locky and Buenos came, of course.

Takeoka and Maria and Zulema, not being Japanese, stayed on at Arribeños as caretakers. They looked after the Hurnys of the Swiss Embassy, who moved in to take care of Japanese interests while we were interned. The Hurnys brought their own Swiss butler.

My rabbit had grown to an enormous size, in keeping with his doberman pen. He had many admirers but finally went to Juan our gardener, who wanted it badly—for a pet, I hoped, and not for his cook pot.

The move was so sudden that I did not have time to say goodbye to all my friends properly. The girls from Michael Ham days I had been seeing less and less, but I did manage to phone Raquel. Mother and I made a point of going to the Esclavas to explain to the nuns and to thank them.

"We'll be praying for you and waiting for you to come back. All your friends, too," said the Mother Superior, taking my hand.

I would miss not only my friends, but the nuns as well.

We left on a special train with the presidential carriage attached to the back for our family use, a very ornate and grand carriage. It brought a smile from Mother, "Gracious, it's like something Queen Victoria might have used."

"Made around that period," said Father. "I am touched that the Argentine government is trying so hard to ease our internment. They were very apologetic, but this had to come sometime."

There were mahogany beds in the two staterooms, and in the bathroom towered a bathtub with rococo gilt taps. The drawing room was an observation car at the very rear and had stuffed velvet armchairs.

We rolled along the countryside to Córdoba, a central province, "where there'll be no suspicion of spying nor agents coming across the border or the sea." Father sounded amused.

There was an endless stretch of *pampas* prairies, flat land with a lone tree offering the sole shade for livestock for miles around. The landscape looked even flatter and vaster close at hand than from the plane from Chile. Herds of cattle and horses roamed the *pampas,* and dotting the landscape was an occasional rotting carcass or skeletons of cattle. It was cheaper to leave them to the hazards of nature than to remove them on these vast *estancia* ranches. I looked to the curving horizon and could see that the world was truly round.

As we climbed towards Córdoba, we weaved through granite sierras and gullies. Once in a while there would be a house near the tracks. They were nothing but desolate shacks, with laundry drying on the bushes and children in torn clothing smiling and waving to the train. I had never seen anyone in rags before and was shocked. There were beggars in Buenos Aires and they wore shabby clothes, but not rags. María had even said that when they came begging to the door, they were insulted if offered anything less than steak.

As the train approached the town of La Falda in Córdoba, we passed a couple of stations, where crowds of curious Cordobeses flashed by. They wanted to see the special train and carriage carrying the Japanese ambassador and his entourage.

At La Falda, police kept back the crowds. Everyone had suntanned, leathery faces. "*Eso debe ser el embajador. Qué linda que es la Señora. Tantos Japoneses! Qué ojos más raros!*" That must be the ambassador. How pretty the Mrs. is. So many Japanese! What funny eyes!

A colonel saluted and clicked his heels. "Your Excellency, I am to accompany you to the Eden Hotel and protect you during your stay there." Twenty men in khaki behind him clicked their heels and saluted. The convoy of some fifty Japanese, including wives and children, was driven through the town to the Eden Hotel. It was better than a parade for the curious onlookers.

The Eden Hotel, true to its name, was a garden of Eden in otherwise barren surroundings. On a plateau, with mountains encircling it in the distance, the forty-year-old Eden Hotel had a genteel but relaxed and informal charm. There was the white, ornate, two-story main building with turrets, like an old hotel in Bournemouth, said Father. There were two closed-up chalets in the garden and two buildings used by the numerous employees in the hotel's heyday, now used mainly by the soldiers. There were the large, mostly barren gardens, with landscaping only in the front, consisting of flowers and a smattering of topiary trees. Behind the main building, eucalyptus trees provided welcome shade. Clusters of cacti of varying sizes dotted the generous amount of gravel that glittered with mica in the strong sun. Elsewhere, nature had taken over except for two tennis courts and the nine-hole golf course, which lay halfway down the plateau. Locky and Buenos would have been in heaven, except that now they were always walked on a leash out of consideration for the other residents, their dogs, and especially their cats.

"A hotel with a small golf course, because we know your Excellency likes golf," Father had been told in Buenos Aires.

Rooms on the upper floor opened onto balconies that encircled the building, rooms on the ground floor to the gardens. Our family was quartered in the left corner upstairs, in order to give us privacy and a view of the front gardens. There was a bedroom for Mother and Father, a room that we used as a breakfast and living room, a tiny turret chamber for Father's study, and my room, which faced the side. In contrast with the outside, the décor inside was Spartan, almost non-existent; I could well believe that in later years the hotel was turned into a sanatorium for tuberculosis sufferers. I liked the turret room best because of its octagonal shape and a spinning wheel, a vestige of the Eden Hotel's happier days.

Life at the Eden Hotel

I walked in the gardens a lot with Locky and Buenos, who strained on their leashes. The abundant mica in the gravel sparkled under the strong mountain sun and there was also mica in the rocks. I chipped some off and wondered whether I could pan for gold.

Once, when I was alone, I stepped on a mound and in sank my right foot. It was a giant anthill; in seconds, black ants that seemed the size of beetles swarmed up my slacks. Screaming, I stomped and brushed them away with both hands and managed to shake them off as I ran from the nest.

"You were lucky to be able to get rid of them before you were bitten; you probably just stepped on the edge," said Father. "In the countryside there are many aggressive insects you wouldn't see in Buenos Aires."

"You must be exaggerating," said Mother.

"I tell you they were as big as grasshoppers, but they didn't bite. I could brush them away and none got under my slacks."

"Ugh. You certainly were lucky. There are *arañas pollitos,* chick spiders, around here too," said Mother. "They are about the size of a man's hand, with hair all over. They're called *arañas pollitos* because they attack chicks and suck their blood."

"I thought they were called *arañas pollitos* because they were as big as chicks," I said.

"Well, whichever—don't turn stones with your hands in your search for gold. Use a stick."

Just then, in flew a swarm of locusts. We all watched through the windows. Big, grasshopper-like things the color of dead grass landed in bunches on trees, bushes, and the ground. More were on the horizon, flying in. They landed on top of each other, forming scatter rugs of locusts.

Once the invasion subsided, we joined the crowd in the front garden to see the creatures close at hand. Maybe frustrated by the sparse vegetation, several locusts flew onto my red and white dress. I swished away the hard and prickly things. One got caught in Mother's hair.

"Eek!"

"Stand still and let me untangle it." Father managed to get it out of her hair as sympathetic bystanders tried to help. "Do you often have locust invasions?" he said to a waiter who had also come out to watch.

"Not so often. Maybe every three years."

"It isn't too bad this time, is it. They look like a lot, but they're in small bunches and they really aren't that many," said Father.

"They're always like this. Sometimes less."

"In China, I hear, when locusts come, the sky becomes black and the crops and everything growing is eaten."

"Not here. They eat a little maybe, but there aren't that many. We burn them."

And so they did the next day, in little heaps. The locusts burned quite well. Must be oily, I thought. I wondered if Masa's grasshoppers were like these.

Everyone came together at lunchtime and dinnertime. I preferred dinnertime, when it was less rushed, people dressed up more, and I could watch them at my leisure.

"These *chinchurines* sausages again." Mother's stomach rebelled against too much oily food.

"I like them better than *pejerreyes* fishes," I said.

The fat, jovial naval attaché came in with his wife; they bowed as they passed our table and sat down. Each family had its set table.

"She's a real Japanese beauty," commented Father.

"Yes, so refined and delicate, quite a contrast from that Mrs. Takayama," agreed Mother.

I looked at Mrs. Takayama at the table next to the naval attaché's. She was very vivacious and always dressed nicely for dinner. Tonight she wore bright green satin with a lot of gold and orange sequinswhereas most of the other women wore simple silk dresses. Three boys, aged two, four, and six, were making a ruckus at the table and Mr. Takayama was trying to keep them quiet. He had a little mustache, looked slightly Argentinean, and spoke fluent Spanish.

"Takayama's all right," said Father. "He's a very smart man, just like Uemura over there."

"Mrs. Uemura's smart too, but she flatters too much."

The Uemuras sat towards the left of the room, their well-behaved baby gulping down the raw meat juice that it was fed. Husband, wife, and baby had pointed, mouse-like faces.

"Colonel Hata's the difficult one."

The military attaché sat at the other end of the dining room. We could clearly hear him saying something to the two assistants who shared his table, since his voice was so loud. He was fat, like the naval attaché, but arrogant rather than jovial.

"Well," said Mother, "I'll tell you who I think are really nice: Mr. Usui and Mr. Nakai. It must be so hard for them, too, leaving their families in Japan."

"Yes, they're men of integrity."

"And the Udagawa family's so nice."

I glanced at the Udagawa family sitting next to the Uemuras. Mr. Udagawa was small, sporty, and dapper, with a gray mustache, while Mrs. Udagawa was plump and motherly and towered over her husband. Twenty-year-old Kikuko was tall like her mother, but with an enviably "sexy" figure. The Udagawas smiled a lot. Kikuko was my friend, for the oldest of all the other girls at the hotel was seven, too much of a baby. Kikuko, however, was never a close friend, not only because of the difference in our ages, but because of her deference to me. I had come to realize that I was always the ambassador's daughter to these embassy people, and that this created a distance. Had I been that to other people too? I hoped not.

"The ladies like it here," said Mother. "They don't have to cook or clean and that makes up for not being free." But Mother, who had never cleaned or cooked at home, was restless. To fill her days, she organized a ladies' bridge group. Father was usually in his study in the mornings, seeing people and "taking care of business." Afternoons he liked to play golf or tennis and evenings he read or played billiards.

"Ayako, come and join us for bridge. Mrs. Kambe can't come today. She's not feeling well. It's a good chance for you to practice what I taught you."

"But Mama, I've only played a little."

"We'll teach you; you can learn as you play. We're very informal anyhow." Mrs. Yanai and Mrs. Iwamura smiled and nodded. "Your deal, Mrs. Yanai. Ayako, you be my partner."

"Pass."

"Were clubs lower than spades?"

"Yes. Were you going to bid clubs?"

"No, I was just wondering. Pass."

"One heart."

"Two no trump."

"Pass."

"Pass."

"???!!!"

Father thought this was a good chance for me to learn golf as well. "You'll be a crack player if you start now."

The pro sold me expensive Bobby Jones clubs and a leather bag. He gave me fifteen lessons, after which, Mrs. Uemura invited me to go around the course with her. She was a good golfer, and not even snapping so many pictures of me could spoil her game. She clicked her camera as I teed off the first hole, topping. The ball bounced along for fifty yards.

"You have a beautiful, natural swing; you'll become a good golfer like your father and mother."

At the second tee shot, also immortalized on film, I duffed.

"You see, you immediately knew what was wrong with the first tee shot and tried to correct it. What a sharp mind for golf you have. You'll be a champion in no time."

I was allowed to have a teacher come in from La Falda to help me keep up with my studies. Srta. Lopez, thirtyish and efficient, came afternoons after she had finished teaching at the local high school. She had thick black expressive eyebrows and skin like leather, and her manner was brusque, but she was a dedicated teacher. She found the blanks in my schooling, where I had just drifted with good conduct, was shocked that I had gotten this far knowing so little and set out to remedy this. Being the only student, I had no chance to be vague and had to study hard, especially algebra and history.

$$(A+B)^2=A^2+2AB+B^2$$
$$(A-B)^2=A^2-2AB+B^2$$

"Who was Rosas? Urquiza? Mitre? Why are they important? Describe the constitution of 1853 and how it affected the nation. What did Rivadavia do? Why is Sarmiento remembered so much today? Who was Roca?"

"Miss Lopez, were you born in La Falda?"

"No. Now let's get back to your history lesson."

Another time, I asked, "Srta. Lopez, do you have a boyfriend?"

"Ayako, you are not concentrating on your algebra." Srta. Lopez did not welcome questions about her private life and was not curious about mine, but she taught her subjects with a passion I had never seen before. She smuggled in related material and books, although that was officially forbidden, as what came in and went out was limited and strictly monitored. As my concentration improved and some of Srta. Lopez's love of her subjects rubbed off on me, her attitude softened. It was amazing how a smile transformed her face more than any cosmetics.

Once I had settled into the routine of life at the Eden Hotel, I also started taking Japanese lessons twice a week. First from a Mr. Hosokawa.

"He majored in Japanese literature," said Father. Mr. Hosokawa also suffered from ulcers. The Japanese lessons were boring, but he was one of two men under thirty at the Eden Hotel. He was sensitive looking and had a pretty wife and a year-old daughter. The other youngish man was a handsome, tall bachelor who was on the tennis courts a great deal and who kept his distance from me. I worked hard at the stupid *kanji* writing to please Mr. Hosokawa, who started explaining the text in detail. I watched him dreamy-eyed. Suddenly, realizing I was not listening at all, he would blush ever so nicely. After six weeks, Mr. Hosokawa said his ulcers had worsened and he quit.

Mr. Shimura, his successor, was fortyish, balding, and wore glasses. He had a delicate white skin that belied his thick hide. I did not like him—I would not have liked anybody who came in Mr. Hosokawa's place. I was rude and nasty to Mr. Shimura. Let him quit, I thought, the sooner the better.

"Have you been bald for a long time?"

Mr. Shimura laughed. He laughed at many of the things I said, and I felt insulted.

"I don't like Mr. Shimura; he laughs at me," I pouted to Father, but Mr. Shimura stayed on. He taught me practical, everyday Japanese, and I learned in spite of myself. He stopped laughing so much and I settled down grudgingly to studying. Sometimes he was brutally frank.

"You're an intelligent girl, so when I say dictation, please do as I say. We all work under your father, so we have to be nice to you, but you don't want to become a spoiled young lady and be unhappy for the rest of your life."

I was angry but saw from his face that he was really concerned, and so I held back my words.

I wrote Mrs. Allen a letter. We had exchanged postcards, and hers had said, "Send me a letter. It's good practice for your English, as I can't go to Cordoba to see you. I promise to write a letter in reply."

Dear Mrs. Allen,

How are you? We are all well. It is already three months since we came to La Falda. The war is going very badly for us. We worry about Masa and the rest of the family, but here we seem so far away from everything.

From my window, I can see the Argentine flag on top of the flagpole in the garden. When we first came, the colonel and twenty soldiers lined up at 8:00 A.M., blew the bugle and stood at attention as the flag was raised. They also guarded us strictly. My golf was very bad in the early days, and once as I was looking for my ball near the fence, a soldier with a rifle appeared from nowhere and asked me what I was doing. When I told him I was looking for my ball, he said all right, but be quick, and he looked around at the mountain range. Papa laughed when I told him this and said the soldier probably thought I planned to escape or was waiting for signals from the surrounding mountain rims, like in a Hollywood Western or a spy movie. Gradually, the number of soldiers in the morning was reduced to sixteen, then nine, with some still buttoning their shirts. The time became later: 8:30, then 9:00. Now only one soldier comes out to raise the flag. Nobody lines up and nobody blows the bugle.

I want to ask you a strange question because I know you always understand. My Japanese teacher here said people have to be nice to me because they work under my father and that I will become spoiled. Is this true? Were people nice to me in Buenos Aires because my father was ambassador? Or did they really like me?

Are you still taking your daily cold baths?

Hoping that you are well,

With love, from Ayako

It took three weeks for Mrs. Allen's promised letter to come.

Dear Ayako,

I was so pleased to receive your long and interesting letter. You have not forgotten your English; in fact, it has improved. You must be reading a lot. I especially enjoyed your vivid description of the soldiers.

I have not written sooner because your question as to why people are nice to other people is a difficult one. Your teacher is partly right. Some people are nice to you just because of your position. I particularly felt that when I became a widow. Those people aren't worth having as friends, so good riddance.

Other people are nice to you because they like you for yourself. But here comes the difficulty. "Yourself" is made up of many qualities for which people like you—or love you: your affectionate ways, your gaiety, your kindness, or your talent in some field. But would they still love you if you lost these qualities, through war, age, some misfortune? Some would, others wouldn't. All this goes beyond "niceness," I'm afraid, but the important thing is to be the kind of person other people would want to be nice to and not worry about what others think of you. Do you understand me?

I would still like to take my daily cold bath, but sad to say, I caught my first cold in six years the other day; so for the moment, the cold baths will have to wait.

Buenos Aires continues to be as beautiful as ever—the Paris of South America—but great changes are taking place in the government and there is a feeling of unrest among the workers.

Please give my best regards to your parents. I pray daily that the terrible war will end soon. Keep in touch dear and take care of yourself.

Fondly,

Phoebe Allen

I smiled over the letter. I thought I understood but wasn't sure. Mrs. Allen sounded less cheerful than usual. Perhaps it was the effect of her cold.

I, on the other hand, had stopped catching colds all the time and had started to sprout up. I had been second from the smallest in my class of twenty, but if I went back now, I'd range in the middle. My figure, too, was starting to fill out, my complexion was no longer sallow, and I was becoming prettier. "Childish for her age" was no longer true; I had started to bloom.

The days were sunny and dry, the evenings cool. The air was so clear that I woke up every morning with my body tingling and feeling good all over. It was the start of another glorious day. I felt guilty that Masa and so many others were suffering the ravages of war in Japan.

Father liked to stretch on the balcony before breakfast, breathing in the La Falda air. "Invigorating. That's why there's a T.B. sanatorium around here—all this clean mountain air. It's certainly done wonders for Ayako's weak lungs."

The End of the War

The war was always very much on Father's and Mother's minds though they tried not to talk about it in front of me. There was nothing but bad news. Germany had surrendered and now Japan was fighting an increasingly hopeless war.

One day in August, there was a great buzz of voices in the living room as I came in. Father, Mr. Nakai, Mr. Usui, and Mother were there. Mother was crying.

My heart contracted. Masa had been killed. We hadn't heard from him at all. "What is it?"

"There's a terrible new bomb, Ayako," said Father. "It seems to have wiped out all of Hiroshima—it's unbelievable. We just heard it on the shortwave."

"Oh." I was relieved it wasn't Masa. How could there be such a bomb? The whole of Hiroshima? How cruel! Where was Hiroshima?

Mother burst out, "The poor, innocent people, all killed, all those children scorched to death. Why are there wars?!"

"Those American monsters! Flame throwers were bad enough, and they call *us* barbarians!" Mr. Nakai banged the table in his agitation.

"Let's try to get more information," said Father. "I'll phone Mr. Hurny of the Swiss Legation." The men rushed out of the room.

Next day, I saw the headlines: "New Bomb Destroys City," "Hiroshima Leveled," "New Bomb to Save Thousands of American Lives," "War to End," "Japan's Defeat Certain." Everyone was stunned to have what they had heard confirmed in print.

"The V-2 rockets of the Germans were nothing compared to this," said Mr. Nakai.

Mr. Usui, usually quiet, said, "I don't want to sound selfish, but I'm so relieved my wife and children moved from Hiroshima to my parents' when I left Japan. They're all in Nagasaki now."

The pall remained over the Eden Hotel as the days passed. Then came August 10th, and the second atomic bomb, this time on Nagasaki.

"City after city! And Mr. Usui's family!" Mother wrung her hands.

"Warfare has changed entirely." Father held his head in his hands. "Japan must realize it has lost."

The Emperor's declaration that Japan would fight no more came on August 15, 1945.

"A sad day for all Japanese, but all the same, what a relief," said Mother.

"You only fight wars that you can win," said Father, "but that's easier said than done. Yes, a sad day for all Japanese. Think of the lives sacrificed."

"I wonder if Masa is alive."

"I think of Masa, my mother, our families, our friends, every day. If I were a Christian, I would pray."

"Are we going back now?" I asked.

"We'll be going back," said Father, "but we'll have to wait till there's a ship to take us."

"When will that be?"

"I don't know. Everything's chaotic now. Not for several months, anyhow."

"How is Mr. Usui?" asked Mother. "The poor man, just when he was so relieved his family had moved from Hiroshima to Nagasaki."

"Usui's devastated. The worst part is not knowing. I tried to console him by telling him that they could have been away and be safe. Thank heavens it's all over."

Three gloomy months passed. All activity seemed to stop at the Eden Hotel. The Hurnys moved out of Arribeños after paying us a farewell visit. The Swiss had finished looking after Japan's interests now that the war was ended.

"Mr. Hurny told me that when the German diplomats were repatriated, Herr Braun fled to Uruguay, then to Portugal with his family," Father told Mother.

"I don't believe it! How selfish and cowardly!"

"I couldn't believe it either. But Mr. Hurny wouldn't make it up. He says the Brauns are now living in luxury in Portugal."

"Not to go back to one's own country, however ravaged it may be!"

"Yes, it's absolutely disgusting."

Sra. Palou wrote to Mother:

Dear Baroness,

I can imagine how especially trying it must be for all of you now. I pray that there will be no more wars. It makes me guilty sometimes to see how peaceful and prosperous Argentina is.

Two weeks ago in the *Nación* newspaper, I saw a notice saying the effects of the Japanese Embassy would be auctioned off and were on view at 1499 Arribeños. I went for sentimental reasons, remembering the pleasant hours spent with you and Ayako. The Japanese lanterns were there in the driveway, though one was chipped. I was surprised when I went in, because much of the furniture were things that had not been there before. They were cheap items brought in and falsely advertised as being used by you. Where did the original things go? Maybe they were sold off first to dealers? Anyhow, there was quite a crowd.

I am enclosing a little lace tablecenter that I managed to buy. I would have gotten you something grander if I could have afforded it, but I recognized the tablecenter as one from the ladies' drawing room.

I imagine you will all be going back to Japan soon. Have a safe voyage, and please tell Ayako not to forget her Spanish.

I have some news of my own. Paulo was born six months ago. I was rather surprised at my age, but he is a delight.

Please give my best regards to His Excellency and to Ayako.

Yours Faithfully,

Ana Maria Palou

Mama fingered the lace for a long time. "I remember buying this with five others like it at Gath & Chaves. How very, very sweet and thoughtful of Mrs. Palou to do this. I never expected it. I am so glad her marriage has been blessed with a child."

Later, Arribeños 1499 was split into twelve lots and sold off.

There was also a letter from María, who had stayed on with Takeoka and Zulema till the Hurnys left. María wrote of the auction, mostly of non-embassy furniture, and added:

There is one bit of bright news in these sad days. Zulema, whom ma'am was always afraid would die an old maid, is to be married. It is a very romantic story, like something out of *Screen Stories,* which Miss Ayako was always asking Takeoka to buy.

The Hurnys brought their own Swiss butler, a quiet, serious man. Who would have thought two such people like he and Zulema would fall in love. They never even flirted. They will be married here, then go to Interlaken, the home of this Kurt Staeger.

Takeoka and your María are going to retire and rest. We've worked hard all our lives and we're both getting old.

Our respects to the Ambassador, and say hello to Ayako, cook and his wife, and to Locky and Buenos. I hope Adachi wasn't as lazy there as he was here.

From,

María

"I'm so glad for Zulema—how elegant to live in Interlaken. I must find her a little present to send with a practical cash gift." Mother smiled for the first time in months. "And I hope dear María won't scold Takeoka too much when they retire. The three have been so faithful to us—what would we have done without them?"

Years later, when I was in college in postwar Japan, I received a call from a *Mainichi* newspaper correspondent. He had just returned from abroad, a special privilege for the defeated Japanese in those days, and as he waited for his train in Zurich, a woman tapped him on the shoulder. "*Konnichiwa*, are you Japanese?" she asked. "I used to work at your embassy in Buenos Aires. Could you look up Baron Tomii and his family when you return to Japan? I used to be their daughter's maid. Tell her to write to me. Here, let me jot down my name and address." He was so surprised and impressed that he looked up our phone number and gave me Zulema's address and message.

Later on still, when I was living in Düsseldorf with my husband and children, I visited Zulema at her home in Interlaken. She lived in a neat chalet in one of the suburbs, where there were many Staegers, relatives all. She had two grown sons, one married and living nearby the other still at home, apprenticing as a carpenter. Her husband was a pleasant man who excused himself after tea to allow us time together. She was surprisingly unchanged—I would have recognized her if we passed each other on the train platform. I was moved to see her after twenty-three years and I think she was too, but she was always a woman of few words. Before I could reacquaint myself enough to express some of the joy I felt, it was time to leave; so much had happened in those twenty-three years that it was difficult to find a common ground on which to explore the bond that we surely shared.

Repatriation

It was nine months after we lost the war that Eden Hotel detainees were told of our return to Japan. Four U.S. freighters would pick us up in Buenos Aires in three weeks, then we'd transfer to a navy transport ship in San Francisco and sail to our homeland. Japanese who were not interned but wished to go back as quickly a possible could also join us.

There was a flurry of activity and I stayed from underfoot as much as possible. One morning I took a shortcut to the staircase from my room by going along the veranda that ran the whole length of the upstairs left side. I had to pass by several rooms. Mr. Usui's French doors were open and revealed him counting a thick wad of bills. Before I could turn my head the other way, he looked up.

"Good morning," I said.

"Good morning," he answered; he then laughed with embarrassment.

I walked on briskly, because nobody liked to be seen counting money. I did not tell everything to Father and Mother those days, as they had so much on their minds, but I told them about Mr. Usui, since they knew him well.

"Poor Usui, probably seeing what provisions he can afford to take back for his family and relatives. I'm hoping against hope his family survived the atomic blast, that they were away."

"Are we taking back provisions for Masa and Grandmother Nakamura—I mean, for family and relatives?" I asked.

"Yes, we are," answered Mother. "The Argentine government has been very kind and are letting us order things. We'll be taking canned goods such as corned beef, butter, powdered milk...I hear there's even such a thing as powdered eggs, but they don't have them here. We'll also be taking sugar, and I've been told salami won't spoil despite the long voyage, so I'm taking several to give to your aunts."

"There's nothing now in Japan, is there," I said. "Everything has been destroyed."

"People are living and people are resourceful. But it will be a great change for you," said Father.

"I'm prepared. I'll work and help."

"Good. That's my girl! When you think of all that those in Japan went through during the war, it will be nothing."

There was no presidential carriage on the way back to Buenos Aires. We were all crowded into two carriages attached to the back of a regular train. At La Falda and other nearby stations, curious crowds unchecked by police pressed their faces to the windows.

"*Ahí están los japoneses, mirá los ojos! Cuál es el embajador? Qué elegante la embajadora y qué mona la chica!*" "There are the Japanese, look at their eyes! Which is the ambassador? How elegant Mme. Ambassador is, and how pretty the girl!" Many smiled and waved. "*Buen Viaje!*" "Have a safe journey!"

Father smiled and waved back. "*Nos gustamos mucho la Argentina. Vamos con buenas memorias.*" "We like Argentina very much. We go back with fond memories."

Mother also smiled and waved. "*Gracias, gracias,* thank you, thank you. Ayako, smile and wave back."

I waved. "*Adiós,* goodbye."

We were to stay five days at a downtown business hotel, the Bourget, and we were free to do what we wanted: last minute shopping, dropping by our former homes, seeing friends…The Argentine government wanted to give the Japanese a little freedom after thirteen months of internment, especially before returning to our war-ravaged homeland.

"Let us not take advantage of their kindness," Father told everyone. "We will act with restraint. No last-minute binges." Father and Mother stayed mostly at the hotel, friends coming to see them there, among them Mr. and Mrs. Imai, with their daughters, as well as Dr. Suzuki, Maria, and Takeoka. Zulema had already left for Interlaken. Kiyoko came with her parents. It seemed such a long time ago that Kiyoko and I had play acted confession and communion—so much had happened since then—so that in our talks, I did not know where to start.

I did go out to the Colegio de las Esclavas with Maria to say goodbye to the nuns and to my school friends. A black flock awaited me in the parlor.

"Dear Ayako." As Mother Superior kissed me I could see Mothers Avelina and Esperanza and Mrs. Allen smiling and making welcoming noises. "How good to see you again. We've all thought of you and prayed a lot for you and your family." Mother Superior stood back and held me at arm's length. "But how tall you've grown—taller than I am. You're a beautiful young lady now!"

I was now 5'4", having sprouted 8 inches in the clear air during the lazy days at La Falda.

Mother Avelina blushed as she always had. "I have to rush back, dear. I'm in the middle of a lesson, but I had to see you." She kissed me and pressed a medal of St. Cecilia into my hands. "You'll take up piano again some day, won't you?" She then dashed away before I could reply.

"Why are you here, Mrs. Allen?"

"That's a nice welcome, Ayako! It's good to see you and all transformed into a young lady. Mother Esperanza told me you would be coming here."

Mother Esperanza smiled. "Phoebe is my sister-in-law, and I know how fond she is of you."

Mother Superior broke in. "You must tell us all about your life at La Falda later, but it's going to be recess time, and you'll be wanting to see your friends. They're in IIA now; that's on the second floor. Sister Felicidad can take you there so you won't lose your way! Meanwhile, we can offer Maria some coffee and convent-baked cookies."

Sister Felicidad, the smiling portress, left me outside IIA. She had a leathery face like the Cordobesas. I watched the last few minutes of class through the glass part of the door. A nun I did not know was writing dates on the blackboard. I could see Zelmira, Olga, Susana, and Luz but no Enriqueta. Maybe she had a cold? Changed schools? They all seemed so childish in their uniforms.

Sister Veronica walked along the corridors, ringing her heavy bell. Recess! Recess!

The unknown nun came out and smiled. Then the girls poured out, chattering, barely giving me curious looks in their hurry to get out. Zelmira rushed past, then Susana and Olga, without recognizing me.

"Zelmira!" I ran after her. "Olga! Susana! Luz!"

They stopped and stared. "Ayako! Is that Ayako!?" We embraced and kissed and laughed. "Girls, it's Ayako!"

A circle formed around me.

"I didn't recognize you; you've changed so!" exclaimed Luz.

"You look so grown up," said Susana.

"She's so pretty," "She's wearing wedgies," "She doesn't look Japanese," "Is that really Ayako?!" "I thought she'd gone back to Japan."

"Are you coming back to school?" asked Olga.

"No, I'm leaving the day after tomorrow for Japan. I came to say goodbye."

"But Japan's all destroyed now. Why don't you stay with us in Argentina?" asked Zelmira.

As I drove away, I could see black and white habits fluttering on the steps.

"Remember to visit our sister house in Tokyo. I will try to send word to Mother Ernestina to help you all she can," Mother Superior repeated.

"God be with you!" Was it Mrs. Allen's voice?

I had rosaries, medals of St. Christopher, the Little Flower, and holy cards bulging from my handbag.

After returning to Japan, Mother Ernestina Ramallo saw to it that I would not forget my Spanish, though there were no classes I could fit into as the school had been temporarily closed before the transition to a new postwar educational system. I still correspond with my friends. I saw Zelmira and Susana in Switzerland and Italy, where they now live, grandmothers both. Luz became a doctor and painter. Susana and Rosamunda Shizue traveled to Tokyo. Raquel is now a grande dame of the Buenos Aires society and is active in volunteer work.

Back at the hotel, I walked to a nearby bookstore to buy some books in Spanish (and maybe *Screen Stories*) for the trip back to Japan. On the street, a young man, lolling against a lamppost, smiled impudently. "*Hola, guapa,*" hiya, good-looking. Another youth poked his face in front of me. "*Japonesita linda!*" Pretty little Japanese girl! I frowned. Strangers talking in such a manner! Fresh! I had more serious things on my mind, like working to help my parents once we returned to Japan.

Father remained mostly secluded in his room, dodging reporters and refusing interviews, although he was happy to see friends. The day before we sailed, however, he decided to venture out to buy two pairs of shoes.

"Would you come with me, Ayako? Then I could stay in the background while you speak like an Argentinean."

So off we went down the street, and I felt very important as I did the talking.

"I would like two pairs of men's shoes, in black, a lace-up pair and a pair of comfortable loafers." I waved in my father's direction to indicate they were for him.

"*Qué tamaño usa el señor, señora?*" What size does the gentleman take, madame?

I was taken aback. It was one thing to be grownup enough to be whistled at but quite another to look old enough to be taken for father's wife or mistress.

"*No sé qué tamaño toma mi padre,*" I don't know what size my father wears, I replied coldly.

We returned to the hotel with two pairs of shoes and Father in a good mood. In the lobby they were playing that music again. Violins tugging at your heartstrings.

"What is it, Father? They're always playing that record. I like it."

"Paganini's Violin Concerto no. 1. A virtuoso piece."

By dinnertime, Father's mood had changed drastically to a rare black one. He barely spoke and only muttered answers as we ate in our rooms, as usual. Afterwards he said, "I think I'll go down to the bar for a while," and he went right out.

"What's the matter with Father? He never goes to the bar. Is it because we're leaving tomorrow?"

"Your father has had more bad news. On top of similar things in the last few days, this was the last straw."

"What?"

"Maybe I shouldn't tell you these things, but you're old enough to keep them to yourself, and you'll understand his mood better if you hear what's been going on."

"I promise I won't tell a soul."

"All right. First, Mr. Tamura has decided not to go back to Japan because he's to marry an Argentine girl."

"Mr. Tamura?" It turned out that he was the handsome bachelor I had noticed at the Eden Hotel.

"It was all right in his case, because she may have been his serious girlfriend and the marriage wasn't just an excuse to stay in Argentina. But yesterday two other men who were to return with us married their former maids and decided to remain behind."

"Who? Who?"

"Never mind. Better that you not know."

"Maybe the maids were pretty."

"I don't know, but one man is said to have a wife back in Japan, maybe children."

"But then he can't marry."

"Shouldn't, but Japan is far away, and things are chaotic there now. The Argentine government is rather lenient about people remaining if they become naturalized."

"No wonder Father wanted a drink."

"That's not all. Right before dinner, he found out that two supposedly upright men, upright enough to be trusted with part of the payroll, disappeared from the hotel, taking the money with them. At least they had the grace to leave a note apologizing and promising to pay back the 'borrowed' amount after they had established themselves."

"I can't believe people do such things; everyone seemed so nice."

"It appears people behave properly when things are going well, but when things don't go the way they want, it's difficult to resist temptation. I didn't think our people at the Eden Hotel would do such things. Neither, I think, did your father. This shows you, you can never tell."

At that moment, Father burst into the room, anger on his face.

"What is the matter? That was a quick drink," said Mother.

Father calmed down a bit. "There was a very pleasant man, and we had a drink together and talked. Then he started asking too many questions, which put me on my guard. I happened to look at the mirror above the bar and there was a microphone hidden on the other side of the counter. One of those damn reporters from a radio station trying to trick me into an interview!"

Five years later, in Tokyo, a letter arrived for Father from La Falda.

Dear Ambassador,

We hope you and your family are well and are not suffering too much in post-war Japan. We apologize again for our disappearing right before going back to Japan, but we had come to love Argentina and wanted to remain. That money saved our lives.

We liked La Falda and started a furniture factory nearby, which is now profitable. We wish to return half of the money we borrowed, which helped us establish ourselves. How and where should we send it? We shall return the rest as soon as we are able to and apologize again to all those affected by our action at the time. We thank you for not having pursued us, for that money was our lifeline…"

It ended with the usual formalities. With a lilt in his step, Father took the letter to the foreign office, and though it was difficult to transfer money in those days, a route was found. Whether the rest was returned I do not know, but I remember that our spirits lifted.

Whenever I hear Paganini, my mind goes back to the seesaw of emotions of those last days in Argentina.

The Maine

Five freighters had made a detour to pick us up. Ours, the SS *Maine,* was one of them. It certainly looked different from the ships we had traveled in: smaller, but comforting rather than stark in its homeliness. It had a lived-in feel. We were now under American rule. How would we, the defeated, be treated?

The naval attaché and Mrs. Yamaguchi were among those on the Maine. The Udagawa family was there also. I was glad that Kikuko would be there to talk to. As for our dogs, Buenos had been given by Mother to the Argentine colonel at the Eden Hotel, but she could not bear to leave Locky, so he came on board with us.

"He's been with us from Canada, and he's such a little dog—he won't eat much," Mother had begged and Father had given in. I was glad; I'd give him my own rations in Japan.

"Welcome on board, sir, ma'am. I'm Captain Kelly. Here are two of my officers, Chief Mate Olsen and our radio operator, Chuck McDonald." Captain Kelly and the others shook hands with Father and Mother. Captain Kelly was grizzled and kindly-looking, Chief Mate Olsen tall, golden-haired, and handsome, and the radio operator paunchy and bald. All three wore crisp navy blue uniforms and white caps.

We were shown to our cabins, cheerful little rooms facing the deck. Later we were given a tour of the *Maine* and saw that some of the officers' rooms were much pokier and below deck. They had given up their rooms for their passengers.

"How very kind of you." Mother was touched.

"Well, it's going to be a long voyage, and we want you folks to be comfortable," said Captain Kelly, who was now wearing khaki slacks and a Hawaiian shirt with a red hibiscus pattern. I found that none of the officers wore their uniform except when in port.

Captain Kelly took a special shine to Locky. Snap, snap went the captain's fingers and Locky, who usually ignored strangers, came over, wagging his tail. "Cute little fella. Going to be hot for you when we pass the equator. I had a mascot: Sheila. Mongrel bitch. Drank beer like a trooper." He laughed. "The girls would give Sheila mug after mug at the…er…bar, and she'd reel up the gangway after me, both of us frothing at the mouth. Ha, ha, ha. But poor little Sheila, she got washed overboard. Never had the heart to keep a dog since." Captain Kelly patted Locky on his head.

At Sao Paulo we anchored offshore.

"We've hit a strike and we can't unload." A week passed, then ten days, before we could dock. Every evening, smart in their uniforms and smiling, the captain and radio operator went ashore on a little boat. The chief mate stayed behind.

The morning we finally sailed from Sao Paulo, Captain Kelly distributed gifts: a bottle of bourbon for Father, a straw hat for Mother, a stuffed dog for me, and sausages for Locky.

"Some souvenirs, since you folks couldn't go ashore," said Captain Kelly.

At Rio de Janeiro, the Sugar Loaf Mountain rose dramatically from the sea, and I watched the cable cars with Father's binoculars. The other freighters had gone ahead without stopping at Rio, and Mother wondered whether this was a tourist stop for us, courtesy of Captain Kelly. I could also see a sandy beach with many bathers. "How beautiful, so much more beautiful than Buenos Aires!"

"The setting is certainly spectacular, but as for the city, Buenos Aires is much more elegant," said Father, taking back his binoculars. "Buenos Aires is rightly called the Paris of South America."

"No place like Rio," said Captain Kelly, looking especially dapper as he walked down the gangway with Chuck McDonald. Perhaps the stop was not entirely altruistic.

When the Maine sailed the next day, the captain distributed shell bracelets to the ladies and we all rattled them appreciatively on our wrists at dinnertime. Afterwards, some of us were invited to the captain's quarters for drinks. Kikuko, who felt seasick much of the time, excused herself, but I went out of curiosity with Father and Mother. Captain Kelly's room was very neat and he had a lot of books, including Jack London's *The Call of the Wild* and *The Sea-Wolf*, Erle Stanley Gardner's *The Case of the Black-Eyed Blonde* and Somerset Maugham's *Short Stories*. I borrowed *The Call of the Wild*.

Chief Mate Olsen didn't drink, and he suggested to me that we go on deck for a breath of fresh air. I was glad for an excuse to get away from Captain Kelly's too-noisy laughter.

I made polite conversation with my best diplomat's-daughter manners. "How long have you been on this ship, Mr. Olsen?"

"Two years. Before that I was in the navy in the Atlantic until I was wounded."

"It must be a very hard, lonely life, being away so much."

"It's not so hard, because I love the sea, though it would be lonely if I had a wife and kids. Don't know how Mike and Chuck stand it. Had a wife once. She left me."

"Oh, I'm so sorry."

"Ran off with my best friend. So I thought I'd see the world and try to forget."

"You must have been to many places."

"Lots of places, mostly in Europe and Latin America, though."

"You haven't been to Japan?"

"No, but now the war's over I hope to get there some day. I'll look you up when I do." He leaned over the railing, arm muscles rippling, blonde hair glistening in the moonlight.

"Oh…er…please do."

"What's your address?" He took out a little black book and turned to me. His eyes were very blue.

"Twenty-seven Higashi Nakano-cho, Higashi Nakano-ku, Tokyo. At least, that's what it used to be. It may be burned down now, I don't know. It's best to ask the foreign office."

"That's a mouthful of an address. Can you write it down? It's too hard for me." He handed me the little black book and a pen and I saw a lot of girls' names and phone numbers.

"What'll you do when you get back to Japan?"

"Oh, I don't know. Go to school or work or help Mother. Everything seems to be in ruins."

"Yeah, it's terrible what ordinary people have to suffer because of the leaders. You might get married, don't you think?"

"Oh no, I'm much too young for that!"

"How old are you?"

"Sixteen."

"Hmm, you look more grownup. Well, girls marry quite young in the Orient. Come here, let me show you something interesting, how to read the stars." He patted the railing beside him. I immediately edged closer to him, because I liked figuring out the stars and knew quite a bit about them. "See that bright star? That's Venus, named for the Goddess of Love." He smelled deliciously of hair tonic.

"I know, and that's the Great Bear, and there's the Dipper with the handle pointed this way." I flailed my right arm. "Though I could never find the Southern Cross, which everyone says is so easy. Can you show me?"

"Why sure, it's right there." He took my left hand, pointed with it, and marked a cross.

At his touch, lightning flashed through my body and I no longer cared about the stars. I flung his surprised hand away. "Where, where? I don't see it."

He grinned at me. "You have to look up to see the stars. Shall we go back inside?"

As I walked in, Mother looked at me quickly and yawned. "It's getting quite late. I think we should go."

Belém was our next stop, up the wide Pará, which poured out to sea at the mouth of the Amazon River. The mouth was a churning swirl of mud, and we continued up a river of mud with jungle on both sides. The silence was eerie and oppressive, only the swishing of the water and an occasional bird's cry breaking the stillness.

"Hell of a town, nothing to do here," grumbled Captain Kelly when we reached Belém.

We sailed on to the Panama Canal. I was finishing *The Call of the Wild* but was eager to see this canal that we had not been able to go through on the way to Argentina.

Captain Kelly came over. "You'll spoil your eyes if you read in the sun. I've just been telling your father and mother that you'll all have to stay in your cabins and keep the portholes closed when we go through the Panama Canal. Sorry, the military are awfully strict. Locky can stay out if he wants to." He shook Locky's paw. And so it was that Locky was the only one on deck from the Eden Hotel group as we went through the locks.

Once in the Pacific, we sailed up the coast of Mexico and the sea turned turquoise and transparent. Myriad fish swam around: big fish, small fish, fish with blue stripes, yellow stripes, and red dots, jelly fish…

"It's so beautiful; you can understand how some people suddenly jump overboard," said Mother.

"Don't be getting any ideas, ma'am." Captain Kelly laughed. "We're almost there, you know."

The night before arriving in San Francisco, the captain and his officers threw a party. "I'm going to miss you folks. You're going to have a hard time in Japan, so here's a few goodies that may come in handy." He gave everyone bags of Butterfingers, Milky Ways, Baby Ruths, and tubes of toothpaste.

"If the members of the occupation forces are half as kind as all of you, Japan is in good hand," said Father in return.

Two winters later, Chief Mate Olsen and Radio Operator McDonald did look us up in Tokyo, en route to Hong Kong. We lived miserably, as did many of our friends, but we managed to invite both of them for *sukiyaki* at Mother's childhood home, which had been turned into a restaurant where we could get a good price. Father and Mother wanted to repay the kindness they had shown us during our voyage and were sorry to hear that Captain Kelly had retired. Chief Mate Olsen wore a tailored dark coat and white silk scarf, which sharply contrasted to the drab clothing in Japan and heightened his blond handsomeness.

San Francisco and the Return to Japan

We were hustled into a building for immigration detainees, joining the others whose freighters had already arrived. Father, Mother, and I were booked into the hospital ward for privacy. Security was tight, with much clanging of doors, Father isolated in a room by himself, Mother and I sharing a room that had two iron beds, a closet, a table, three chairs, two bibles, and little else. It was all very impersonal. We were confined to our room, with forays to a deserted lobby-like area for exercise, and we saw Father only once a day, at dinnertime in our room. The meals were brought on trays.

The *San Francisco Chronicle* arrived with breakfast the next morning. American papers were so interesting, especially the advertisements, though *Screen Stories* didn't face serious competition. Mother and I were told we were welcome to visit the chaplain, and so we went, having little else to do.

That evening, over turkey and beans and potatoes, which I thought delicious, Mother, who didn't share my enthusiasm, described the meeting with the chaplain to Father. "It was nice to walk around a bit, though there wasn't much to see, mostly corridors and closed doors. The chaplain wasn't a man as I had expected, but a little old lady in black who was very kind and patient. She asked us if we were comfortable. We spoke a little about our voyage, and since I didn't want to talk about our families back in Japan, the chaplain read us parts of the bible, about the good Samaritan and then the crucifixion."

"She gave us a beautiful black leather bible with gold around the edges of the pages to take with us to Japan," I added.

"You've probably read the bible already in Spanish"

"No, when we went to Mass on Feast Days we were read bits, but in class we used the catechism more than the bible."

"The chaplain looked pained when I told her I didn't believe in an afterlife," said Mother.

"Maybe you needn't have told her that if she was being so kind," put in Father.

"She asked me, you see, so I had to admit that, like most Japanese, I didn't believe in another life."

"You and I don't, but it certainly would be a consolation if we did when we lose loved ones, like a son…"

I looked at Father, whose voice had cracked for a moment.

"Yes, I think she was trying to give us strength, as you say, and it was kind of her, but I couldn't help feeling impatient…" Mother bit her lip and furrowed her eyebrows as she always did when she was worried. She darted a glance at me then smiled brightly at Father. "Anyway, what did you do today?"

"I was called out and questioned much of the day. That's to be expected. They want to know about our activities in Argentina, especially during the war: how we conducted our affairs, whom we saw, what others did—I think all the men are being questioned."

"Anything about our families back in Japan?"

"They're mum on that. Probably they don't know, as they're not interested in that as much as the political aspects of everyone's stay in Argentina. When Japan has suffered so much, I don't want to ask such personal questions that only concern us."

"Isn't Masa safe?" I exclaimed. Father and Mother hadn't spoken about him, and I had taken for granted that he was all right. Otherwise, they would have said something, wouldn't they? Now that I thought about it, we hadn't talked about what a happy reunion we'd have in Japan after so many years apart.

"Masa's probably waiting for us. I don't think he would have been drafted yet, and he was always a healthy boy. The Swiss Legation did send us word when your Grandmother Tomii died of pneumonia, and we haven't heard anything since, so no news is good news." Father tried to sound cheerful. "It's always nice to be 100% sure though."

Mother sighed. "Do you know when we'll be sailing?"

"No word of that yet."

The third evening, Father came in, angry.

"What's the matter?" Mother asked quickly.

"The CIA questioned me today, and the way they grilled me, you'd think I was a criminal. They asked me all sorts of impertinent questions, made false allegations and eventually accused me of spying!"

"No!"

"Not only that, but they said Toda—you know that reporter—had informed them of my activities. I thought it was one of their tactics again, to make me say something rash in my anger, but then they brought in Toda himself and I couldn't believe it. He accused me of being involved in all sorts of things; it was mostly nonsense, but with just enough truth to make me sound bad. Like we had a transmitter on the roof and that I was transmitting all sorts of secret information from the embassy. We did have a transmitter we used for catching shortwave broadcasts and for sending messages back and forth, so of course it sounded bad."

"He always nursed a grudge against you because you didn't give him all the hot news first, as he wanted."

"Well, I must admit, his attitude—that reporters were almighty—rubbed me the wrong way, but he's Japanese after all, and you don't turn false informer on your government's representative!"

"Maybe it's every man for himself now. He does this, lands you on the blacklist when the CIA's looking for a villain, and gets into the good graces of the Occupation Forces when we all return."

"I don't want to even think such things. This involves patriotism. My, you've grown cynical, Hide."

"Just realistic. In spite of all the glamour, I never liked diplomatic life. You did."

"I loved it—and still do. To play even a small part in my country's future while meeting interesting people in different lands and enjoying my work—I've been very lucky. It's not diplomatic life that's bad, it's the war that's changed values."

"Well, diplomatic life as you know it is over. I always wanted a little house of our own and a private life. If you're blacklisted, I'm not too proud to go out and be the breadwinner."

"Oh, come, come, let's not be melodramatic. Ayako will think I'm finished." Father managed to laugh, putting a potato into his mouth. "There's one piece of good news anyhow: we're sailing tomorrow at four in the afternoon on an army transport ship, so you'd better start packing."

"Goodness! Why didn't you say so before! Not that we have much to pack."

I was outraged for Father, for I never doubted that he was telling the truth. I hadn't seen this reporter, but if I ran into him, I'd give him a piece of my mind, knock his teeth out, kill him if I could. I felt bitter. All those people not wanting to return to the hardships of a defeated Japan before we boarded in Buenos Aires, then all this lying for the sake of revenge and ambition. How appearances deceived. People who seemed nice, were not really nice. You could not trust anyone.

The *General Taylor* was very different from Captain Kelly's freighter. This army transport ship was a huge gray thing with all the men in one large, windowless dormitory with bunk beds four high. The women and children were put in another windowless room with more spacious bunk beds. Military police guarded the exits. Inner cabins with bunk beds for four were given to our family, the Udagawas, the Yamaguchis, and the military attaché and his assistants. Military police stood at the doors of the deck reserved for us Japanese.

Kikuko was seasick again, so I kept mostly to myself, reading or walking Locky on deck, spotting breaching whales four times and playful porpoises racing the ship. These were moments of joy in an otherwise gray voyage, though the weather couldn't have been gray all the time. I pampered Locky, brushing him, feeding him, walking him on his red leash, and also gathering his droppings with paper and throwing the bundle overboard. I learned to gauge the wind properly after a messy error.

One foggy evening, I had just finished hurling Locky's droppings from the deserted deck when I heard a voice behind me.

"You certainly pay a lot of attention to a mere dog."

I turned to see a pale, short young man glaring at me through his glasses. I vaguely remembered his face from the Eden Hotel—so there had been three and not two youngish men, though I'd never noticed him till today. "Locky's been with us for more than seven years. He's like a member of the family."

"Drivel. To take back a dog to a Japan short of food is insulting. You know they might eat him over there. Just because your father was ambassador you get all these privileges: a better room, a dog…have you seen the hole the rest of us sleep in?"

I was speechless with surprise.

"After we go back, I'm going to help make a better society where everyone is equal and where there won't be special privileges for anyone!"

"How dare you talk like that."

"And nobody like you is going to turn up her nose at me. You don't even know what kind of life the masses are leading. You're still young, so I'm just trying to warn you out of kindness that you'd better change if you don't want to be crushed underfoot when you get back to Japan. Your father's too old to change—we'll have no use for people like him—but you still have a chance. You can open your eyes and learn."

"But you worked under my father!"

He made an impatient gesture. "Don't you understand? I'm telling you for your own sake because I think it's a pity you should waste your life. Mix more with the rest of us to learn what our lives are like. Be friendly to us instead of spending all your time with that dog." He disappeared into the fog.

I returned to my bunk in a state of indignation. He would never have dared to talk like that of Father if he were still ambassador. I had not even known of that squirt's existence till that day. Maybe he was having a nervous breakdown. He was right, though, that I shouldn't have taken a dog back to war-torn Japan—even Father had said so until he had finally given in to my begging and Mother's pleading. I looked at Locky, spread-eagled on the floor. How could I leave him behind? I saw Locky running and sliding on the skating rink at Daly Avenue, chasing cats with Buenos at Arribeños. I'd give him some of my own rations in Japan.

I kept the encounter to myself; my parents had enough worries. Father was writing in his diary at our desk, and Mother was in the bunk beneath mine, probably reading. Privileges. Yes, we did enjoy privileges, but that was because Father was cleverer, worked better, was more important than that squirt, so why shouldn't there have been privileges? Was that wrong? Were there many people like that brusque man in Japan? I knew that we were going back to a very different world. Was he just sick?

Ten days after leaving San Francisco, the *General Taylor* anchored off Uraga harbor amidst a flurry of suppressed excitement in our group. We could see the Japanese coast and I sensed both expectation and foreboding around me.

"Not Yokohama? "Mother was puzzled.

"Seems not."

"Now we'll know about Masa and the rest of the family." Mother kept her eyes down.

"Yes, that's been uppermost in my mind, though surely, they are all right."

I had not realized how very worried Father and Mother really were, and my stomach tensed as I tried to remain upbeat.

A boat pulled up alongside with American military police and Japanese officials who came on board, our first link with this new Japan.

The official in charge bowed. "Welcome back, Your Excellency. We appreciate all your efforts to serve your country and the hardships you have endured during internment."

"My efforts were useless, and it was all of you in Japan who underwent untold hardships. We from Argentina hope to share a fraction of your burden on our return, and we look forward to working hard to building a new Japan."

"You will not be able to recognize Tokyo, Your Excellency. It is a mass of rubble and hovels. We supplement our meager rations by going to the countryside with knapsacks containing whatever we can barter and beg the farmers for sweet potatoes. To ease your return till you become accustomed to war-torn Japan, Your Excellency, we are issuing you and your family some special rations." He proudly produced a twelve-inch brown paper bag.

"This is most kind of you, but we do not want any special privileges. I no longer represent Japan. I'm just an ordinary citizen. Ayako, can you hold this? Perhaps you would allow me to give it to some of the smaller children on board?"

"But I was told to give this to you and your family especially. The others have been given their own rations."

"Oh well, in that case, thank you very much. As you say, we are not used to conditions in Japan, and these provisions will be a great help."

I knew that according to Japanese custom, you were not supposed to open gifts immediately, but I was curious to know what all the fuss was about. Nobody took notice of me in the back, so I pried open one corner of the bag and saw what looked like brown dog biscuits. They were as hard as stone. Afterwards, I learned it was a very filling emergency ration, aptly called *kata-pan,* or "hard bread." It would keep forever. I pricked up my ears as I heard the official say, "…your honored son."

"I have good news and bad news to convey. First, the good news: your honored son is well and is waiting for you at the pier."

Mother gasped and her hand flew to her heart. "He's alive!"

Father smiled broadly.

"And eagerly waiting for you with all the family news, which unfortunately I don't have. Now for the bad news: your home was razed to the ground in the big air raid of March this year."

"If our son is alive, if the family is together, we can live anywhere. Thank you so much for telling us. Wondering whether he was all right had been foremost in our minds, but I didn't want to seem selfish and ask. You wouldn't happen to know about family left in our homeland by other Japanese on this ship, would you?"

"I'm afraid not, Your Excellency, but we will help them find out after we land."

The tugboats pulled the *General Taylor* with maddening slowness towards land, and I noticed for the first time how clear and blue the sky was; it was a beautiful day. A smattering of Japanese men in drab clothing, most of it worn olive army wear, waited at the pier. Everyone had a greenish complexion, and there wasn't even one fat man.

"There he is, that's him!" Mother waved wildly.

"Masa! Masa!" Father used his hat as a banner.

A thin, pale, handsome youth in a khaki shirt looked our way. He resembled old pictures of Father, before he was married.

"Here, Masa, here!" The three of us were laughing and waving like mad.

Father's sunny smile, that same smile, lit up Masa's pinched face, as he waved back to us. In that world of defeat, we came together in delirious joy. It was the happiest day of our lives.

In Tokyo we shared the hardships of defeat: meager food and meager housing (including the embarrassment of fleas jumping under skirts when friends visited). But we were also swept up in the exhilaration of starting something new in a world destroyed, in the energy that comes from determination and hope.

Father, blacklisted when his name came up for foreign minister in the Ashida cabinet, turned to the world of business as advisor to Yawata Steel and to Hazama Gumi. Now he had more time to read the books he loved.

Mother, an experienced shopper, worked in the section for Occupation Forces of the Takashimaya Department store as a customer advisor and personal shopper. At home, she learned to cook rice for the first time in her life.

My brother, who was to be drafted for suicide subs in what turned out to be the final weeks of the war, made up for lost time by studying hard in the Structural Engineering department at the Tokyo Imperial University. I can still see him reading for an exam by the light of a street lamp in the falling snow during one of our frequent power failures.

After a year of high school, I studied at the Sacred Heart University in a class of twenty-eight, as women could now go to university under the new educational system. We wore old-model U.S. Women's Marine Corps uniforms, which I later spotted in the Smithsonian. At home, I tried to make myself useful by ironing (badly), cleaning, and helping in as many household chores as I could, for it broke my heart to see my glamorous parents in such reduced circumstances. I could not understand how they remained so cheerful.

My long childhood gave way to a short adolescence on returning to Japan. Nowadays, childhood and innocence are much more short lived and differ greatly from mine so long ago. Yet, the needs of a child remain the same, and I shall always be grateful to my parents for giving me an ordinary childhood under the cloud of war in our not-so-ordinary lives.

Ayako with Locky and rabbit. Zulema and gardener's daughter in background. Rear garden of 1499 Arribeños, Belgrano, Buenos Aires, Buenos Aires, 1943.

Baron Tomii in full dress uniform, outside his bedroom. 1499 Arribeños, Buenos Aires, 1942.

Internees and administrators. Baron and Baroness Tomii (front middle), Ayako (standing, front middle). Front steps of the Eden Hotel, La Falda, Cordoba. 1945.

0-595-29800-1

Printed in Great Britain
by Amazon